MEMOIRS
OF THE
LIFE
OF THE LATE
GEORGE FREDERIC HANDEL

Da Capo Press Music Reprint Series

MUSIC EDITOR
BEA FRIEDLAND
Ph.D., City University of New York

MEMOIRS
OF THE
LIFE
OF THE LATE
GEORGE FREDERIC HANDEL

By JOHN MAINWARING

New Foreword By
J. MERRILL KNAPP

DA CAPO PRESS • NEW YORK • 1980

Library of Congress Cataloging in Publication Data

Mainwaring, John, d. 1807.
  Memoirs of the life of the late George Frederic
Handel.

  (Da Capo Press music reprint series)
  Reprint of the 1760 ed. published by R. and J.
Dodsley, London.
  "A catalogue of his works, and observations upon
them": p.
  1. Händel, Georg Friedrich, 1685-1759.
  2. Handel, Georg Friedrich, 1685-1759—
Bibliography. 3. Composers—Biography. I. Title.
[ML410.H13M2 1980] 780'.92'4 [B] 80-14096
ISBN 0-306-76042-8

This Da Capo Press edition of
Memoirs of the Life of the Late George Frederic Handel
is an unabridged republication of
the first edition published in London in 1760.

Published by Da Capo Press, Inc.
A Subsidiary of Plenum Publishing Corporation
227 West 17th Street, New York, N.Y. 10011

Manufactured in the United States of America

(V)

FOREWORD

T HIS LITTLE BIOGRAPHY OF HANDEL, published anonymously in 1760, one year after the composer's death, has always been a landmark of its kind. It is probably the "first on any one composer in the English language."[1] There had obviously been short accounts of composers published in dictionaries and other sources previous to the mid-eighteenth century; but this book was apparently the first to attempt a complete life of a creative musician in English.

Moreover, there has always been a certain amount of mystery about its author. Why did the Rev. John Mainwaring,

---

[1] Charles Cudworth, *Handel* (London: Clive Bingley, 1972), p. 45.

(VI)

formerly of St. John's College, Cambridge, later Rector of Church Stretton, Salop, Shropshire, and then Professor of Divinity at Cambridge, not attach his name to the volume? Was he afraid of criticism or was he merely following the fashionable practice of the day in publishing anonymously and then letting everybody in that small world hear by rumor that he was the author? Who induced the reverend gentleman to write a biography of the then best-known musical figure in England when Mainwaring apparently had not even known Handel and received his information second-hand from John Christopher Smith, Jr., Handel's amanuensis in the declining years of his life?

The implication in Chrysander's Handel biography[2] is that Mainwaring was only a young theological student at the time (aged 25) and wanted to capitalize immediately on Handel's fame, much as certain writers do today with presidents,

[2] Friedrich Chrysander, *G.F. Händel,* Vol. I, Introduction (Leipzig: Breitkopf und Härtel, 1858), p.v.

(VII)

movie stars, and other public figures, most
of whom have not even been laid to rest.
Deutsch,[3] however, our present authority
on most details in Handel's life, says that
Mainwaring was born in 1724, not 1735,
and thus considerably older than a student when he published his book. Moreover, no records disclose when Mainwaring was openly acknowledged as the author. As late as 1785, Charles Burney in
his "Sketch of the Life of Handel,"[4]
makes no mention of Mainwaring's name
in connection with the *Memoirs;* nor do
the various reviews with excerpts from the
book which appeared earlier in 1760.[5] The
same is true of Johann Mattheson's German translation of it,[6] issued in 1761 with

[3] Otto Erich Deutsch, *Handel, A Documentary
Biography* (New York: W.W. Norton, 1955; Da
Capo reprint, 1974), pp.842-843.

[4] *An Account of the Musical Performances in
Westminster-Abbey and the Pantheon in Commemo-
ration of Handel* (London: no publ., 1785; Da Capo
reprint, 1979), p.2.

[5] Deutsch, p.842.

[6] *Georg Friedrich Händels Lebensbeschreibung,*
reprinted H. and E.H. Mueller von Asow (Vienna:
Franz Perneder, 1949).

(VIII)

some very important corrections and comments about Handel's early life that Mattheson, who had known Handel intimately in Hamburg, was in a position to make. Even the Earl of Shaftesbury, who had followed Handel's career in London and was acquainted with him personally, did not refer to Mainwaring when he made further corrections and comments about the volume in late 1760.[7]

In spite of these mysteries, the little book is really more than a biography. It also contains a general catalogue of Handel's works, and there is a separate section which makes observations on them. Deutsch[8] says the catalogue was compiled by James Harris, a cousin of the Earl of Shaftesbury, and the "Observations," a considerable part of the volume (49 pages out of 208), written by a Richard Price (Deutsch cites no source for this information). This third part seems to be a mixture of Mainwaring and Price, if quota-

[7] Deutsch, pp.844-848.
[8] Deutsch, p. 842.

tion marks are any indication. At any rate, the whole book to this day has remained a foundation stone of Handel studies on which every subsequent biographer has relied to some extent.

Although some of the facts and the chronology in it have since been disproved, the book is written in a refreshingly breezy manner, and it is still a pleasure to read.[9] It is rather a relief to find the eminent "Mr. Handel" coming alive through its pages with no heavy apparatus of footnotes and documentation to weigh him down. We have to smile at many of the pretty little stories which have been passed down over the years, probably through a combination of Smith's faulty memory and Mainwaring's too vivid imagination. Some of them are: the seven-year-old

[9] *The Monthly Review* or *Literary Journal* of June, 1760 reported the writing to be "free, easy, and not inelegant. If it wants anything, it is that laboured correctness which distinguishes the works of those who are Writers by profession; but whose works, at the same time, are often equally destitute of certain graces . . ."

(X)

Handel pursuing his father's carriage on foot when the latter was making his way to Weissenfels to see the Duke; the smuggling by young Handel of a clavichord into the family attic against his father's command (no mean trick if true); Handel sitting on Ariosti's lap in Berlin; the "service of plate" from the Medici after the success of *Rodrigo* in Florence; the presumed love affairs with Italian female singers; and several other events for which there is no verification or proof. Yet it can be firmly said that there is probably a grain of truth in most of these stories, elaborated or changed as they may have been. Mainwaring could not have invented them out of whole cloth. They came largely from John Christopher Smith, Jr., Handel's closest associate at the end of his life, who undoubtedly heard countless reminiscences from the aging composer.

Perhaps the most interesting part of the book are the "Observations" on Handel's music at the end. Here is a piece of musical criticism and contemporary aesthetics that has considerable value apart from biography.[10] Most of the diary and press comments on Handel's music during his lifetime were a string of adjectives with little specific musical substance. But the author or authors here deal directly with Handel's style—and not uncritically, particularly his Italian operatic writing. They compare him with such composers as Vinci and Pergolesi and complain that his instrumental accompaniment often overpowers his vocal line—a familiar remark from the next generation who felt that Handel and Bach were too old-fashioned toward the end of their careers and had not kept up with the new taste of the time. They find his greatest strokes in the oratorio choruses, particularly *Messiah,* but also single out for special mention several operatic arias and recitatives which transcend any matter of current style. They take considerable space in discussing the independent Italian duets and trios which are a submerged part of the Handelian repertoire today and deserve

[10] Peter Kivy, "Mainwaring's *Handel:* Its Relation to English Aesthetics," *JAMS,* Vol XVII/2 (Summer, 1964), 170-178.

far more attention than they usually get. Altogether this section gives a penetrating insight into what certain informed English musical taste of the 1760s may have been.

The first few sentences with which the anonymous reviewer of the June, 1760 *Monthly Review* begins his article is as good a summary of the volume as any:

"Altho' the History of a Musician may be considered, by many, as the least important, and the least generally interesting, species of Biography; yet the life of so great a Genius as the late Mr. Handel, who was, in truth, the very Shakespeare of Music, cannot be altogether an indifferent subject to the admirers of that exquisite science; and more especially to those who are proficients in it. They in particular, will be pleased with these Memoirs of Mr. Handel, not only on account of the anecdotes relating to the incidents of that great man's life, but also for the sake of the Writer's ingenious observations on his truly admirable compositions."[11]

J. MERRILL KNAPP
Princeton University
June 1980

[11] *The Monthly Review,* Vol. XXII (London: R. Griffiths, 1760), p.471.

MEMOIRS

OF THE

LIFE

OF THE LATE

George Frederic Handel.

Anno ætat:56.

MEMOIRS

OF THE

LIFE

OF THE LATE

GEORGE FREDERIC HANDEL.

To which is added,

A CATALOGUE of his WORKS,

AND

OBSERVATIONS upon them.

Εγω δ᾽ οιδα μὲν, ὡς αἱ ὑπερβολαὶ μεγέθυς Φύσει ἥκιςα
καθαρχί. Τὸ γὰρ ἐν παντὶ ἀκριβὲς, κίνδυν☞ ζμι-
κρότη1☞. LONGINUS.

- - - - - - - - -
Untwifting all the Chains that tie
The hidden Soul of Harmony.
MILTON.

LONDON:

Printed for R. and J. DODSLEY, in *Pall-Mall*.
M. DCC. LX.

(1)

MEMOIRS

OF THE

LIFE

OF

George Frederic Handel.

GEORGE FREDERIC HANDEL was born at HALL, a city in the circle of Upper-Saxony, the 24th February 1684, by a fecond wife of his father, who was an eminent furgeon and phyſician of the fame place, and above ſixty when his ſon

B   was

was born. He had also one daughter by the same wife. HANDEL always retained the strongest affection for this sister, to whose only daughter, *i. e.* his niece now living, he bequeathed the greatest part of his ample fortune.

While he was yet under seven years of age, he went with his father to the Duke of Saxe-Weisenfels. His strong desire to pay a visit to his half-brother, a good deal older than himself, (for we have before observed that he was the issue of a second marriage) and at that time valet de chambre to the Prince, was the occasion of his going. His father intended to have left him behind, and had actually set out without him. He thought one of his age a very improper companion when he was going to the

the court of a Prince, and to attend
the duties of his profeſſion. The
boy finding all his ſolicitations ineffectual, had recourſe to the only
method which was left for the ac-
compliſhment of his wiſh. Having
watched the time of his father's
ſetting out, and concealed his intention from the reſt of the family,
he followed the chaiſe on foot. It
was probably retarded by the rough-
neſs of the roads, or ſome other ac-
cident, for he overtook it before it
had advanced to any conſiderable
diſtance from the town. His father, greatly ſurpriſed at his cou-
rage, and ſomewhat diſpleaſed with
his obſtinacy, could hardly reſolve
what courſe to take. When he
was aſked, how he could think of
the journey, after ſuch a plain re-
fuſal had been given him; inſtead
of anſwering the queſtion, he re-

newed

newed his intreaties in the moſt
preſſing manner, and pleaded in
language too moving to be reſiſted.
Being taken into the chaiſe, and
carried to court, he diſcovered an
unſpeakable ſatisfaction at meeting
with his brother above-mentioned,
whom till then he had never ſeen.

This was not the firſt inſtance of
the father's ill ſucceſs, when he
judged it expedient to oppoſe or
over-rule his ſon's inclinations.
This matter demands a more particular explication, before an account can properly be given of
what afterwards paſſed at the court
of Weiſenfels.

From his very childhood HANDEL
had diſcovered ſuch a ſtrong pro-
penſity to Muſic, that his father,
who always intended him for the
ſtudy

ftudy of the Civil Law, had reafon
to be alarmed. Perceiving that this
inclination ftill increafed, he took
every method to oppofe it. He
ftrictly forbad him to meddle with
any mufical inftrument; nothing of
that kind was fuffered to remain in
the houfe, nor was he ever permitted to go to any other, where fuch
kind of furniture was in ufe. All
this caution and art, inftead of re-
ftraining, did but augment his paffion. He had found means to get a
little clavichord privately convey'd
to a room at the top of the houfe.
To this room he conftantly ftole
when the family was afleep. He
had made fome progrefs before Mufic had been prohibited, and by his
affiduous practice at the hours of
reft, had made fuch farther advances, as, tho' not attended to at

that

that time, were no flight progno-
ftics of his future greatnefs.

And here it may not be unplea-
fing to the reader, juft to remind
him of the minute and furprifing
refemblance between thefe paffages
in the early periods of HANDEL's
life, and fome which are recorded
in that of the celebrated monfieur
Pafcal †, written by his fifter. Nothing could equal the bias of the
one to Mathematics, but the bias
of the other to Mufic : both in
their very childhood out-did the
efforts of maturer age : they purfued their refpective ftudies not only
without any affiftance, but againft
the confent of their parents, and
in fpite of all the oppofition they
contrived to give them.

We

† Tycho Brahe is another inftance of the
like kind.

We left our little traveller juſt on his arrival with his father at the Duke of Saxe-Weiſenfels. In ſuch a ſituation it was not eaſy to keep him from getting at harpſichords, and his father was too much engaged to watch him ſo cloſely there as he had done at home. He often mentioned to his friends, this uncontroulable humour of his ſon, which he told them he had taken great pains to ſubdue, but hitherto with little or no ſucceſs. He ſaid it was eaſy to foreſee, that if it was not ſubdued very ſoon, it would preclude all improvements in the ſcience for which he intended him, and wholly diſconcert the plan that had been formed and agreed on for his education.

The reaſonableneſs of ſuch apprehenſions every one admitted, in

caſe

cafe it was determined to adhere to the fcheme above-mentioned. But the prudence of adhering to it was doubted by many. It was obferved with reafon, that where Nature feemed to declare herfelf in fo ftrong a manner, refiftance was often not only fruitlefs, but pernicious. Some faid, that, from all the accounts, the cafe appeared fo defperate, that nothing but the cutting off his fingers could prevent his playing; and others affirmed, that it was a pity any thing *fhould* prevent it. Such were the fentiments and declarations of the Doctor's friends in regard to his fon. It is not likely they would have had any great effect, but for the following incident, which gave their advice all the weight and authority it feems to have deferved.

It

It happened one morning, that while he was playing on the organ after the fervice was over, the Duke was in the church. Something there was in the manner of playing, which drew his attention fo ftrongly, that his Highnefs, as foon as he returned, afked his valet de chambre who it was that he had heard at the organ, when the fervice was over. The valet replied, that it was his brother. The Duke demanded to fee him.

After he had feen him, and made all the inquiries which it was natural for a man of tafte and difcernment to make on fuch an occafion, he told his phyfician, that every father muft judge for himfelf in what manner to difpofe of his children; but that, for his own part, he could not but confider it

as

as a fort of crime againft the public and pofterity, to rob the world
of fuch a rifing Genius!

The old Doctor ftill retained his
prepoffeffions in favour of the Civil
Law. Though he was convinced
it was almoft become an act of neceffity to yield to his fon's inclinations (as it feemed an act of duty to
yield to the Prince's advice and authority) yet it was not without the
utmoft reluctance that he brought
himfelf to this refolution. He was
fenfible of the Prince's goodnefs in
taking fuch notice of his fon, and
giving his opinion concerning the
beft method of education. But he
begged leave humbly to reprefent
to his Highnefs, that though Mufic
was an elegant art, and a fine
amufement, yet if confidered as an
occupation, it had little dignity,

as

3

as having for its object nothing better than mere pleaſure and entertainment: that whatever degree of
eminence his ſon might arrive at
in ſuch a profeſſion, he thought
that a much leſs degree in many
others would be far preferable.

The Prince could not agree with
him in his notions of Muſic as a
profeſſion, which he ſaid were much
too low and diſparaging, as great
excellence in any kind entitled men
to great honour. And as to profit,
he obſerved how much more likely
he would be to ſucceed, if ſuffered
to purſue the path that Nature and
Providence ſeemed to have marked
out for him; than if he was forced
into another track to which he had
no ſuch bias; nay, to which he
had a direct averſion. He concluded with ſaying, that he was far
from

from recommending the ſtudy of Muſic in excluſion of the Languages, or of the Civil Law, provided it was poſſible to reconcile them together : what he wiſhed was, that all of them might have fair play; that no violence might be uſed, but the boy be left at liberty to follow the natural bent of his faculties, whatever that might be.

All this while he had kept his eyes ſtedfaſtly fixed on his powerful advocate; and his ears were as watchful and attentive to the impreſſions which the Prince's diſcourſe made upon his father.

The iſſue of their debate was this : not only a toleration was obtained for Muſic, but conſent for a maſter to be employed, who ſhould forward and aſſiſt him in

his

his advances on his return to Hall.
At his departure from Weifenfels,
the Prince fill'd his pockets with
money, and told him, with a fmile,
that if he minded his ftudies, no
encouragements fhould be wanting.

The great civilities which he had
received at the court of Weifenfels,
the profperous iffue of the debate
juft mentioned, but efpecially the
friendly and generous difmiffion
which the Prince had given him,
were often the fubject of his thoughts.
Thefe fortunate incidents ferved to
foment that native emulation, and
to inflame that inbred ambition,
which, even at this early period it
was eafy to difcover in him.

The firft thing which his father
did at his return to Hall, was to
place him under one ZACKAW, who
was

was organist to the cathedral church. This person had great abilities in his profession, and was not more qualified than inclined to do justice to any pupil of a hopeful disposition. HANDEL pleased him so much, that he never thought he could do enough for him. The first object of his attention was to ground him thoroughiy in the principles of harmony. His next care was to cultivate his imagination, and form his taste. He had a large collection of Italian as well as German music: he shewed him the different styles of different nations; the excellences and defects of each particular author; and, that he might equally advance in the practical part, he frequently gave him subjects to work, and made him copy, and play, and compose in his stead. Thus he had more exercise, and

more

more experience than ufually falls to the fhare of any learner at his years.

ZACKAW was proud of a pupil, who already began to attract the attention of all perfons who lived near Hall, or reforted thither from diftant quarters. And he was glad of an affiftant, who, by his un-common talents, was capable of fupplying his place, whenever he had an inclination to be abfent, as he often was, from his love of company, and a chearful glafs. It may feem ftrange to talk of an affiftant at feven years of age, for he could not be more, if indeed he was quite fo much, when firft he was committed to the care of this perfon. But it will appear much ftranger, that by the time

he

he was nine he began to compofe the church fervice for voices and inftruments, and from that time actually did compofe a fervice every week for three years fucceffively. However, it muft not be forgot, that he had made fome progrefs at home, before his father began to be alarmed, and, in confequence thereof, had forbid him to touch any mufical inftrument : that, after this fevere prohibition, he had made further advances at ftolen intervals by his practice on the clavichord; and after that had made the moft of his moderate ftay at the court of Weifenfels, where he found many inftruments, and more ad-mirers.

We have already hinted at fome ftriking coincidencies of life and character, which are found in him,
and

and the famous Paſcal. In this place we may juſt obſerve, that the latter, at the age of twelve compos'd a treatiſe on the propagation of founds, and at ſixteen another upon conic ſections.

From the few facts juſt related it is eaſy to gueſs, that from the time of HANDEL's having a maſter in form, the Civil Law could have had no great ſhare of his attention. The bent of his mind to Muſic was now ſo evident, and ſo prevailing, that the Prince's advice was punctually followed. No further endeavours were uſed to alter or correct it. The conſequence of this full liberty was foon perceived, the pupil ſurpaſſed the maſter, the maſter himſelf confeſſed his ſuperiority. HALL was not a place for ſo aſpiring a youth

C

to be long confined to. During
this interval of three or four years,
he had made all the improvements
that were any way confiftent with
the opportunities it afforded ; but
he was impatient for another fituation, which would afford him better, and fuch a one at length prefented itfelf. After fome confulta-
tions, BERLIN was the place agreed
on. He had a friend and relation
at that court, on whofe care and
kindnefs his parents could rely. It
was in the year 1698 that he went
to Berlin. The Opera there was
in a flourifhing condition, under
the direction of the King of Pruf-
fia, (grandfather of the prefent)
who, by the encouragement which
he gave to fingers and compofers,
drew thither fome of the moft eminent from Italy, and other parts.
Among thefe were BUONONCINI and

ATTILIO, the fame who afterwards
came to England while HANDEL
was here, and of whom the former was at the head of a formidable oppofition againft him. This
perfon was in high requeft for his
compofitions, probably the beft
which that court had known. But
from his natural temper, he was
eafily elated with fuccefs, and apt
to be intoxicated with admiration
and applaufe. Though HANDEL
was talk'd of as a moft extraordinary player on the harpfichord
for one fo young, yet on account
of his years he had always confidered him as a mere child. But
as people ftill perfifted in their
encomiums, it was his fancy to try
the truth of them. For this end
he compofed a Cantata in the chro-
matic ftyle, difficult in every refpect, and fuch as even a mafter,

C 2   he

he thought, would be puzzled to play, or accompany without some previous practice. When he found that he, whom he had regarded as a mere child, treated this formidable composition as a mere trifle, not only executing it at sight, but with a degree of accuracy, truth, and expression hardly to be expected even from repeated practice; — then indeed he began to see him in another light, and to talk of him in another tone.

ATTILIO, somewhat his inferior as a composer, was a better performer on the harpsichord, and, from the sweetness of his temper, and modesty of his character, was much more beloved as a man. His fondness for HANDEL commenced at his first coming to Berlin, and continued to the time of his leaving it.

He

He would often take him on his
knee, and make him play on his
harpſichord for an hour together,
equally pleaſed and ſurprized with
the extraordinary proficiency of ſo
young a perſon; for at this time
he could not exceed thirteen, as
may eaſily be ſeen by comparing
dates. The kindneſs of ATTILIO was
not thrown away; as he was always welcome, he never loſt any
opportunity of being with him, or
of learning from him all that a
perſon of his age and experience
was capable of ſhewing him. It
would be injuſtice to BUONONCINI
not to mention his civilities to HAN-
DEL, but they were accompanied
with that kind of diſtance and re-
ſerve, which always leſſen the value of an obligation, by the very
endeavour to enhance it. The
age of the perſon to be obliged

ſeems

seems to remove all suspicion of
rivalship or jealousy. One so young
could hardly be the object of either;
and yet from what afterwards happened, such a notion may appear to
some persons not altogether destitute of probability. Those who
are fond of explaining former pas-
sages by subsequent events, would
be apt to say, that the seeds of
enmity were sown at Berlin; and
that though they did not appear
'till the scene was changed, they
waited only for time and occasion
to produce them.

Thus much is certain, that the
little stranger had not been long at
court before his abilities became
known to the King, who frequently sent for him, and made
him large presents. Indeed his Majesty, convinc'd of his singular
endow-

endowments, and unwilling to lose the opportunity of patronizing so rare a genius, had conceived a design of cultivating it at his own expence. His intention was to send him to Italy, where he might be formed under the best masters, and have opportunities of hearing and seeing all that was excellent in the kind. As soon as it was intimated to HANDEL's friends (for he was yet too young to determine for himself) they deliberated what answer it would be proper to return, in case this scheme should be proposed in form. It was the opinion of many that his fortune was already made, and that his relations would certainly embrace such an offer with the utmost alacrity. Others, who better understood the temper and spirit of the court at Berlin, thought

C 4   this

this a matter of nice speculation,
and cautious debate. For they well
knew, that if he once engag'd in
the King's service, he must remain
in it, whether he liked it, or not;
that if he continued to please, it
would be a reason for not parting
with him; and that if he happened
to displease, his ruin would be the
certain consequence. To accept an
offer of this nature, was the same
thing as to enter into a formal engagement, but how to refuse it
was still the difficulty. At length
it was resolved that some excuse
must be found. It was not long
before the King caused his inten-
tions to be signified, and the answer was, that the Doctor would
always retain the profoundest sense
of the honour done to him by the
notice which his Majesty had been
graciously pleased to take of his
son;

fon; but as he himfelf was now grown old, and could not expect to have him long with him, he humbly hoped the King would forgive his defire to decline the offer which had been made him by order of his Majefty.

I am not able to inform the reader how this anfwer was relifhed by the King, whom we may fuppofe not much accuftomed to refufals, efpecially of this fort. Such an incident made it improper for HANDEL to ftay much longer at the court of Berlin, where the more his abilities fhould be known and commended, the more fome perfons would be apt to fift and fcrutinize the motives of his father's conduct.

Many

Many and great were the compliments and civilities which he received on his leaving Berlin. As yet he had been but twice from home, and both times had received such marks of honour and distinction, as are seldom, if ever, paid to one of his age and condition. On his return to Hall, he began to feel himself more, to be conscious of his own superiority, to discover that spirit of emulation, and passion for fame, which urged him strongly to go out into the world, and try what success he should have in it. His acquaintance with the eminent masters at Berlin had opened his mind to new ideas of excellence, and shewn him in a more extended view the perfections of his art. After his friends had refused such offers as the King had made him, he never could

could endure the thought of ſtay-
ing long at home, either as a pupil
or ſubſtitute to his old maſter ZAC-
KAW. He had heard ſo high a
character of the ſingers and compoſers of Italy, that his thoughts
ran much on a journey into that
country. But this project required
a longer purſe than he was as yet
provided with, and was therefore
ſuſpended till ſuch time as it could
be compaſſed without hazard or
inconvenience. In the mean while,
as his fortune was to depend on
his ſkill in his profeſſion, it was
neceſſary to conſider of ſome place
leſs diſtant, where he might employ his time to advantage, and
be ſtill improving in knowledge
and experience. Next to the Opera
of Berlin, that of HAMBURGH was
in the higheſt requeſt. It was reſolved

folved to fend him thither on his own bottom, and chiefly with a view to improvement. It was a wife refolution not to engage him too early with a view to profit. How many parents have murdered the fine talents of their children by weakly facrificing that liberty and independency, which are effential to their exertion ! This confideration had ever been attended to by his friends while he was under their direction. And it is very remarkable that HANDEL, when he came to act for himfelf, conftantly purfued the fame falutary maxim. In the fequel of his life he refufed the higheft offers from perfons of the greateft diftinction ; nay, the higheft favours from the faireft of the fex, only becaufe he would not be cramped or confined by particular attachments.

His father's death happened not long after his return from Berlin. This event produced a confiderable change for the worfe in the income of his mother. That he might not add to her expences, the firft thing which he did on his arrival at Hamburgh, was to procure fcholars, and obtain fome employment in the orcheftra. Such was his induftry and fuccefs in fetting out, that the firft remittance which his mother fent him he generoufly returned her, accompanied with a fmall prefent of his own. On this occafion it is but juftice to obferve, that the fame generous regard for thofe with whom he had any natural or accidental

dental connection, appeared in the
later, as well as in the earlier periods of his life. But a very few
years before his death, being informed that the widow of ZACKAW
was left ill provided for, he sent
her money more than once. He
would have done the same by her
son, for whose welfare he appeared
to be equally anxious; but the af-
furances he received, that all such
fervices would only furnish him
with opportunities of increasing
those fottish habits he had contracted, with-held his hand.

Before we advance any farther
in his history, it is neceffary fome
accounts should be given of the
Opera at Hamburgh, as well as
fome character of the compofer and
fingers.

The

The principal fingers were CON-
RATINI and MATHYSON. The latter
was fecretary to Sir Cyril Wych,
who was refident for the Englifh
court, had HANDEL for his mufic-
mafter, and was himfelf a fine player
on the harpfichord. MATHYSON was
no great finger, for which reafon
he fung only occafionally ; but he
was a good actor, a good compofer of leffons, and a good player
on the harpfichord. He wrote
and tranflated feveral treatifes. One
that he wrote was on Compofition.
He had thoughts of writing the
life of HANDEL many years before
his death. Had he purfued this defign, he would have had advantages beyond what we can pretend
to, *i. e.* ampler and frefher materials ; at leaft, for fo much of the
life as had then elapfed. All that
is

is here intended, is to give a plain, artless account of such particulars as we have been able to learn, and such only as we have reason to believe authentic. To return to our narration.

CONRATINI excelled greatly both as an actress and a singer. KEYSAR did the same as a composer, but being a man of gaiety and expence, involved himself in debts, which forced him to abscond. His Operas, for some time, continued to be performed during his absence. On his disappearing, the person who before had played the second harpsichord, demanded the first. This occasioned a dispute between him and HANDEL, the particulars of which, partly for the sake of their singularity, and partly on account

count of their importance, may
deferve to be mentioned.

On what reafons HANDEL ground-
ed his claim to the firft harpfichord
I do not underftand: he had played a violin in the orcheftra, he
had a good command on this inftrument, and was known to have
a better on the other. But the
older candidate was not unfit for
the office, and infifted on the right
of fucceffion. HANDEL feemed to
to have no plea but that of natural
fuperiority, of which he was confcious, and from which he would
not recede. This difpute occafioned parties in the Opera-houfe.
On the one fide it was faid, with
great appearance of reafon, that
to fet fuch a boy as HANDEL over
a perfon fo much his fenior, was
both unjuft and unprecedented.

On the other, it was urged with
fome plaufibility, that the Opera
was not to be ruined for puncti-
lios ; that it was eafy to forefee,
from the difficulties KEYSAR was
under, that a Compofer would foon
be wanted, but not fo eafy to find
a perfon capable of fucceeding him,
unlefs it were HANDEL. In fhort,
matters (they faid) were now at
that pafs, that the queftion, if fairly ftated, was not who fhould conduct the Opera, but whether there
fhould be any Opera at all.

Thefe arguments prevailed ; and
he, to whom the firft place feemed
of courfe to be due, was conftrain-
ed to yield it to his ftripling-com-
petitor. But how much he felt the
indignity, may be gueffed from the
nature and degree of his refent-
ment ; more fuited to the glowing
temper

temper of an Italian, than to the phlegmatic conftitution of a German : For, determined to make HANDEL pay dear for his priority, he ftifled his rage for the prefent, only to wait an opportunity of giving it full vent. As they were coming out of the orcheftra, he made a pufh at him with a fword, which being aimed full at his heart, would for ever have removed him from the office he had ufurped, but for the friendly *Score*, which he accidentally carried in his bofom ; and through which to have forced it, would have demanded all the might of Ajax himfelf.

Had this happened in the early ages, not a mortal but would have been perfuaded that APOLLO himfelf

D 2   had

had interpofed to preferve him, in
the form of a mufic-book.

From the circumftances which
are related of this affair, it has
more the appearance of an affaffi-
nation, than of a rencounter : if
the latter, one of HANDEL's years
might well be wanting in the cou-
rage, or the fkill to defend himfelf :
if the former, fuppofing him capable of making a defence, he could
not be prepared for it.

How many great men, in the very
dawning of their glory, have been
planted, like him, on the very verge
of deftruction ! as if Fortune, jealous of Nature, made a fhew of
facrificing her nobleft productions,
only to remind her of that fupre-
macy to which fhe afpires !

Whatever

Whatever might be the merits of the quarrel at firſt, HANDEL ſeemed now to have purchaſed his title to precedence by the dangers he had incurred to ſupport it. What he and his friends expected, ſoon happened. From conducting the performance, he became Compoſer to the Opera. KEYSAR, from his unhappy ſituation, could no longer ſupply the Manager, who therefore applied to HANDEL, and furniſhed him with a drama to ſet. The name of it was ALMERIA, and this was the firſt Opera which he made. The ſucceſs of it was ſo great, that it ran for thirty nights without interruption. He was at this time not much above fourteen: before he was quite fifteen, he made a ſecond, entitled FLORINDA; and ſoon after, a third called NERONE, which were heard with the ſame applauſe. It

D 3   never

never was his intention to settle at
Hamburgh ; he told the Manager,
on his firſt application to him, that
he came thither only as a traveller,
and with a view to improvement :
that till the Compoſer ſhould be at
liberty, or till ſome other ſucceſſor
or ſubſtitute could be found, he
was willing to be employed, but was
reſolved to ſee more of the world
before he entered into any engagements, which would confine him
long to any particular place. The
Manager left that matter for him
and his friends to determine ; but
ſo long as he thought proper to be
concerned in the Opera, he promi-
ſed him advantages at leaſt as great
as any Compoſer that had gone before him. This indeed was no more
than what intereſt would readily
ſuggeſt to a perſon in his ſituation :
for good houſes will always afford
good

good pay, to all who bear a part in the performance; and efpecially to that perfon, whofe character and abilities can enfure its fuccefs.

At the time that ALMERIA and FLORINDA were performed, there were many perfons of note at Hamburgh, among whom was the Prince of Tufcany, brother to John Gafton de Medicis, Grand Duke. The Prince was a great lover of the art for which his country is fo renowned. HANDEL's proficiency in it, not only procured him accefs to his Highnefs, but occafioned a fort of intimacy betwixt them: they frequently difcourfed together on the ftate of Mufic in general, and on the merits of Compofers, Singers, and Performers in particular. The Prince would often lament that HANDEL was not acquainted with thofe of Italy;

D 4   fhewed

fhewed him a large collection of Italian Mufic ; and was very defirous he fhould return with him to Florence. HANDEL plainly confeffed that he could fee nothing in the Mufic which anfwered the high character his Highnefs had given it. On the contrary, he thought it fo very indifferent, that the Singers, he faid, muft be angels to recommend it. The Prince fmiled at the feverity of his cenfure, and added, that there needed nothing but a journey to Italy to reconcile him to the ftyle and tafte which prevailed there. He affured him that there was no country in which a young proficient could fpend his time to fo much advantage ; or in which every branch of his profeffion was cultivated with fo much care. HANDEL replied, that if this were fo, he was much at a lofs to conceive how

how fuch great culture fhould be
followed by fo little fruit. However, what his Highnefs had told
him, and what he had before heard
of the fame of the Italians, would
certainly induce him to undertake
the journey he had been pleafed to
recommend, the moment it fhould
be convenient. The Prince then
intimated, that if he chofe to return with him, no conveniences
fhould be wanting. HANDEL, without intending to accept of the favour defigned him, expreffed his
fenfe of the honour done him. For
he refolved to go to Italy on his own
bottom, as foon as he could make
a purfe for that occafion. This
noble fpirit of independency, which
poffeffed him almoft from his childhood, was never known to forfake
him, not even in the moft diftrefs-
ful feafons of his life.

During

During his continuance at Hamburgh, he made a confiderable number of Sonatas. But what became of thefe pieces he never could learn, having been fo imprudent as to let them go out of his hands.

Four or five years had elapfed from the time of his coming to Hamburgh, to that of his leaving it. It has already been obferved, that inftead of being chargeable to his mother, he began to be ferviceable to her before he was well fettled in his new fituation. Tho' he had continued to fend her remittances from time to time, yet, clear of his own expences, he had made up a purfe of 200 ducats. On the ftrength of this fund he refolved to fet out for Italy.

The

The number of schools and aca-
demies for Music subsisting in the
different quarters of this country,
and the vast encouragements afforded to those who excel in the Art,
have long conspired, with all the advantages of constitution and climate,
to render it the most eminent part
of the world for its Composers, Singers, and Performers. As each of
these separate classes hath a style and
manner peculiar to itself, so there
are some things well worth observ-
ing, which are common to them
all. And a foreigner, who would
make a figure in the profession,
ought to observe them with the
greater exactness, because they are
such as cannot be marked, or written, or even described. So little
are they to be learnt by rule, that
they are not unfrequently direct
viola-

violations * of rule. I am at a lofs
what to call them, unlefs they are
certain beauties and delicacies in
fentiment and *expreffion*, which are
only to be catched from long ha-
bit, and attentive obfervation. Tho
they feem, at firft fight, to be next
to nothing, yet how much depends
upon

* The very firft anfwer of the Fugue in the
overture for Mucius Scævola, affords an inftance of this kind. Geminiani, the ftricteft
obferver of rule, was fo charmed with this direct tranfgreffion of it, that, on hearing its
effect, he cried out, Quel femitono (meaning
the f. fharp) vale un mondo!

The younger Scarlatti often makes a happy ufe of thefe licences, though fome think he
ufes them too often. It is certain that they
ought not to be ufed without great caution
and judgment. They would not be tolerated
but for thofe great and ftriking effects which
they are found to produce, when under the
management of a great Mafter.

It is needlefs to obferve the exact analogy
which Poetry and Painting bear to Mufic in
refpect to thefe licences, to which the flender
company of great Genius's feem to claim an
exclufive privilege.

upon them, we may judge from
the terms in which the Italians
ufually defcribe them, viz. *è quel
tantino, chi fa tutto.*

Indeed, from the beft information which we can get of the ftate
of the Art in its different ftages and
periods, it fhould feem as if no people ever attained to fuch excellency
in Vocal Mufic, or poffeffed fo extenfive a command over the paffions and affections as the Italians.✝

The

✝ Here I am fenfible that I have the ABBE
DU BOS directly againft me. So ftrong are
his prejudices in favour of the Mufic of his
own nation, that he makes no fcruple of fetting LULLI above all the Italian Mafters.
Voſſius having declared his reafons for prefer-
ing the ancient to the modern Muſicians;
and the ABBE not conceivng any of either claſs
fit to be compared with his countryman, de-
fires his readers to confider the queſtion in the
following view:

" Qu'on fe figure donc quelle comparaiſon
Voſſius auroit faite des CANTATES, & des So-
NATES

The paſſionate admirers of HAN-
DEL's ſtyle, are apt to confound this
characteriſtic excellence of *theirs*
with

NATES des Italiens, avec les Symphonies &
les Recits de LULLI, s'il les eût connus, lorſ-
qu'il écrivit le livre dont je parle."

And might we not aſk the ABBE DU BOS
what he conceives that the ſame learned Critic
would have thought on this ſubject, had he
lived to ſee the very elegant and ſenſible *Lettre
ſur la Muſique Françoiſe* [par J. J. Rouſſeau,
Citoyen de Genéve] in which it is proved, almoſt to a demonſtration, as well from the in-
tractable genius of the language, as from the
perverted taſte of the nation, that the French
are never likely to have any Muſic which an
impartial and competent judge of the Art
would endure. This is ſo true, that what is
tolerable in LULLI himſelf, is borrowed from
thoſe very Italians ſo lightly valued. The advantages which he drew from his acquaintance
with CORELLI, will not be forgot, any more
than the return which he made him by raiſing
a faction againſt him, and driving him from
Paris. Theſe are no good arguments of the
greatneſs of his mind, notwithſtanding he was
thought worthy of being exalted to the rank
of a Stateſman and Privy-counſellor.

After

with that effeminacy of tafte, which proceeds from the vain attempt to command thofe ftrong feelings of the foul without genius, art, or judgment. They do not confider the advantages he derived from his thorough acquaintance with the Italian

After all that is here infinuated to his difadvantage as a Mufician, I am far from thinking that he was deftitute of talents, and lefs reafon is there for believing this of his great fucceffor Monfieur RAMEAU. It is the more to be lamented that fortune fhould have thrown them where the beft parts which nature could beftow would be fure of receiving a wrong biafs; as well from the untoward caft of the language (equally unfit both for Mufic and Poetry) as from the corruption of the national tafte, to whatever ulterior caufes this latter may be afcribed.

'Tis true, Mr. ADDISON, at the end of his laft paper upon Operas, has not only vindicated, but commended the tafte of the French for Mufic. But in vain does the ingenious ABBE endeavour to avail himfelf of his authority. For though all men will agree with him that the Mufic of every country fhould

(48)

Italian Masters, to whose delicate and beautiful melody he added indeed still higher touches of expression, at the same time that he united it with the full strong harmony of his own country. †

We

be adapted, as fas as may be, to the pronunciation and accent of its inhabitants; yet doth it by no means follow, that the pronunciation and accent of every people is equally suited to the purposes of Music; the unalterable principles of which, nay, those of Architecture and Painting also, he resolves at once into the inconstant, arbitrary decisions of custom and caprice. See Spect. Vol. I. N°. 29. p. 121. 12mo Edit. The excellence of Mr. ADDISON both as a man and a writer, hath almost consecrated his mistakes; and the influence of his judgment in the present case is the more to be feared, because it is much better known, that he had an exceeding fine taste for the polite arts in general, than that he had a very imperfect knowledge of Music in particular; yet the poetry in his Opera of ROSAMOND is as strong a proof of this, as his idea of the French compositions.

† A more particular account of the Italian Music is given in the beginning of the observations subjoined to the life.

2

We left him juſt on the point of
his removal to Italy ; where he arrived ſoon after the Prince of Tuſ-
cany. FLORENCE, as it is natural
to ſuppoſe, was his firſt deſtina-
tion ; for he was too well known
to his Highneſs to need any other
recommendations at the court of
the Grand Duke, to whoſe palace
he had free acceſs at all ſeaſons,
and whoſe kindneſs he experienced
on all occaſions. The fame of his
abilities had raiſed the curioſity of
the Duke and his court, and rendered them very impatient to have
ſome performance of his compoſing. With leſs experience, and
fewer years to mature his judgment, he had hitherto ſucceeded
to the utmoſt extent of his wiſhes.
But he was now to be brought to
the trial in a ſtrange country, where

E the

the ftyle was as different from that
of his own nation, as the manners
and cuftoms of the Italians are from
thofe of the Germans. Senfible as
he was of this difadvantage, his
ambition would not fuffer him to
decline the trial to which he was
invited. At the age of eighteen
he made the Opera of RODRIGO,
for which he was prefented with
100 fequins, and a fervice of plate.
This may ferve for a fufficient teftimony of its favourable reception.
VITTORIA, who was much admired
both as an Actrefs, and a Singer,
bore a principal part in this Opera.
She was a fine woman, and had for
fome time been much in the good
graces of his Serene Highnefs. But,
from the natural reftlefnefs of certain hearts, fo little fenfible was fhe
of her exalted fituation, that fhe
conceived a defign of transferring
her

her affections to another person.
HANDEL's youth and comeliness,
joined with his fame and abilities in
Music, had made impressions on
her heart. Tho' she had the art
to conceal them for the present,
she had not perhaps the power,
certainly not the intention, to ef-
face them.

The nature of his design in tra-
velling made it improper for him
to stay long in any one place. He
had stayed near a year at Florence,
and it was his resolution to visit
every part of Italy, which was any
way famous for its musical performances. VENICE was his next re-
sort. He was first discovered there
at a Masquerade, while he was playing on a harpsichord in his visor.
SCARLATTI happened to be there,
and affirmed that it could be no one

but

but the famous Saxon, or the devil.
Being thus detected, he was strongly importuned to compofe an Opera. But there was fo little profpect
of either honour or advantage from
fuch an undertaking, that he was
very unwilling to engage in it. At
laft, however, he confented, and in
three weeks he finifhed his AGRIP-
PINA, which was performed twenty-
feven nights fucceffively ; and in a
theatre which had been fhut up for
a long time, notwithftanding there
were two other Opera-houfes open
at the fame time ; at one of which
GASPARINI prefided, as LOTTI did
at the other. The audience was fo
enchanted with this performance,
that a ftranger who fhould have
feen the manner in which they were
affected, would have imagined they
had all been diftracted.

The

The theatre, at almoſt every pauſe, reſounded with ſhouts and acclamations of *viva il caro Saſſo-ne !* and other expreſſions of approbation too extravagant to be mentioned. They were thunder-ſtruck with the grandeur and ſublimity of his ſtile : for never had they known till then all the powers of harmony and modulation ſo cloſely arrayed, and ſo forcibly combined.

This Opera * drew over all the beſt ſingers from the other houſes. Among the foremoſt of theſe was the famous VITTORIA, who a little before HANDEL's removal to Ve-

E 3   nice

---

* It ſeems that French Horns, and other wind-inſtruments as little known to the *Ita-lians*, were introduced on this occaſion. I believe they never had heard them before, as accompaniments to the voice.

nice had obtained permiſſion of the grand Duke to ſing in one of the houſes there, At AGRIPPINA her inclinations gave new luſtre to her talents, HANDEL ſeemed almoſt as great and majeſtic as APOLLO, and it was far from the lady's intention to be ſo cruel and obſtinate as DAPHNE,

Having mentioned the moſt ma-terial occurrences at Venice, we are now to relate his reception at ROME. The fame of his muſical atchievements at Florence and at Venice had reached that metro-polis long before him. His arrival therefore was immediately known, and occaſioned civil enquiries and polite meſſages from perſons of the firſt diſtinction there. Among his greateſt admirers was the Cardinal OTTOBONI, a perſon of a refined taſte,

tafte, and princely magnificence.
Befides a fine collection of pictures
and ftatues, he had a large library
of Mufic, and an excellent band
of performers, which he kept in
conftant pay. The illuftrious
CORELLI played the firft violin,
and had apartments in the Cardinal's palace. It was a cufto-
mary thing with his eminence to
have performances of Operas, Oratorios, and fuch other grand compofitions, as could from time to
time be procured. HANDEL was
defired to furnifh his quota; and
there was always fuch a greatnefs
and fuperiority in the pieces compofed by him, as rendered thofe of
the beft mafters comparatively little
and infignificant. There was alfo
fomething in his manner fo very
different from what the Italians
had been ufed to, that thofe who

were

were feldom or never at a lofs in performing any other Mufic, were frequently puzzled how to execute his. CORELLI himfelf complained of the difficulty he found in playing his Overtures. Indeed there was in the whole caft of thefe compofitions, but efpecially in the opening of them, fuch a degree of fire and force, as never could confort with the mild graces, and placid elegancies of a genius fo totally diffimilar. Several fruitlefs attempts HANDEL had one day made to inftruct him in the manner of executing thefe fpirited paffages. Piqued at the tamenefs with which he ftill played them, he fnatches the inftrument out of his hand; and, to convince him how little he underftood them, played the paffages himfelf. But CORELLI, who was a perfon of great modefty

and

and meeknefs, wanted no convic-
tion of this fort; for he ingenuoufly declared that he did not underftand them; *i. e.* knew not how
to execute them properly, and give
them the ftrength and expreffion
they required. When HANDEL
appeared impatient, *Ma, caro Saf-
fone* (faid he) *quefta Mufica è nel
ftylo Francefe, di ch' io non m' in-
tendo* *.

A little incident relating to Co-
RELLI, fhews his character fo ftrongly, that I fhall be excufed for re-
citing it, though foreign to our
prefent purpofe. He was requefted
one evening to play, to a large and
polite company, a fine Solo which
he

* The Overture for IL TRIONFO DEL TEM-
PO was that which occafioned CORELLI the
greateft difficulty. At his defire therefore he
made a fymphony in the room of it, more in
the Italian ftyle.

he had lately compofed. Juft as he was in the midft of his performance, fome of the number began to difcourfe together a little unfeafonably; Corelli gently lays down his inftrument. Being afked whether any thing was the matter with him? Nothing, he replied, he was only afraid that he interrupted converfation. The elegant propriety of this filent cenfure, joined with his genteel and good-humoured anfwer, afforded great pleafure, even to the perfons who occafioned it. They begged him to refume his inftrument, affuring him at the fame time, that he might depend on all the attention, which the occafion required, and which his merit ought before to have commanded.

Hitherto Handel has chiefly been confidered, if not wholly, in the

the quality of Compofer. We fhall now have occafion to enter into his character as a Player or Performer. And it muft not be forgot, that, though he was well acquainted with the nature and management of the violin; yet his chief prac- tice, and greateft maftery was on the organ and harpfichord.

When he came firft into Italy, the mafters in greateft efteem were ALESSANDRO SCARLATTI, GASPA- RINI, and LOTTI. The † firft of thefe he became acquainted with at Cardinal OTTOBONI's. Here alfo he became known to DOMINI- CO SCARLATTI, now living in Spain, and author of the celebrated lef- fons.

† This perfon (*i. e.* the elder SCARLATTI) was author of an Opera entitled, PRINCIPESSA FIDELE, which is reckoned a chéf-d'oeuvre in its kind. He alfo made feveral Cantatas very highly efteemed by the judges of Mufic.

fons. As he was an exquifite player on the harpfichord, the Cardinal was refolved to bring him and HANDEL together for a trial of fkill. The iffue of the trial on the harpfichord hath been differently reported. It has been faid that fome gave the preference to SCARLATTI. However, when they came to the Organ there was not the leaft pretence for doubting to which of them it belonged. SCARLATTI himfelf declared the fuperiority of his antagonift, and owned ingenuoufly, that till he had heard him upon this inftrument, he had no conception of its powers. So greatly was he ftruck with his peculiar method of playing, that he followed him all over Italy, and was never fo happy as when he was with him.

HAN-

HANDEL ufed often to fpeak of this perfon with great fatisfaction; and indeed there was reafon for it; for befides his great talents as an artift, he had the fweeteft temper, and the genteeleft behaviour. On the other hand, it was mentioned but lately by the two PLAS [the famous Haut-bois] who came from Madrid, that SCARLATTI, as oft as he was admired for his great execution, would mention HANDEL, and crofs himfelf in token of veneration.

Though no two perfons ever arrived at fuch perfection on their refpective inftruments, yet it is remarkable that there was a total difference in their manner. The characteriftic excellence of SCAR-
LATTI

LATTI feems to have confifted in a certain elegance and delicacy of expreffion. HANDEL had an uncommon brilliancy and command of finger : but what diftinguifhed him from all other players who poffeffed thefe fame qualities, was that amazing fulnefs, force, and energy, which he joined with them. And this obfervation may be applied with as much juftnefs to his compofitions, as to his playing.

While he was at Rome he was alfo much and often at the palaces of the two Cardinals, COLONNA, and PAMPHILII. The latter had fome talents for Poetry, and wrote the drama of IL TRIONFO DEL TEMPO, befides feveral other pieces, which HANDEL fet at his defire, fome in the compafs of a fingle evening,
and

and others extempore. † One of
thefe was in honour of HANDEL
himfelf. He was compared to
ORPHEUS, and exalted above the
rank of mortals. Whether his Eminence chofe this fubject as moft
likely to infpire him with fine conceptions, or with a view to difcover
how far fo great an Artift was
proof againft the affaults of vanity,
it is not material to determine.
HANDEL's modefty was not however
fo exceffive, as to hinder him from

com-

---

† The ABBE DU BOS, fpeaking of that general turn for Mufic for which the Italians
from the higheft to the loweft have ever been
remarkable, continues thus,— Ils fçavent encore chanter leurs amours dans des vers qu'ils
compofent fur le champ, & qu'ils accompag-
nent du fon de leurs inftruments. Ils les touchent, fi non avec délicateffe, du moins avec
affez de jufteffe : c'eft ce qui s'apelle *impro-
vifer.*
I

complying with the defire of his illuftrious * friend.

As he was familiar with fo many of the Sacred Order, and of a per-fuafion fo totally repugnant to theirs, it is natural to imagine that fome of them would expoftulate with him on that fubject. For how could thefe good catholicks be fuppofed to bear him any real regard, without endea-vouring to lead him out of the road to damnation ? Being preffed very clofely on this article by one of thefe exalted Ecclefiaftics, he re-plied, that he was neither qualified, nor difpofed to enter into enquiries of this fort, but was refolved to die a member of that communion, whether true or falfe, in which he was born and bred. No hopes ap-pearing

* This expreffion will not be thought too ftrong by thofe who know what fincere efteem and cordial regard he attracted from perfons of the higheft diftinction.

pearing of a real converfion, the
next attempt was to win him over
to outward conformity. But neither arguments, nor offers had any
effect, unlefs it were that of con-
firming him ftill more in the principles of proteftantifm. Thefe applications were made only by a few
perfons. The generality looked upon him as a man of honeft, though
miftaken principles, and therefore
concluded that he would not eafily
be induced to change them. While
he was at Rome he made a kind of
Oratorio entitled, Resurrectione,
and one hundred and fifty Cantatas, befides Sonatas and other
Mufic.

From Rome he removed to
Naples, where, as at moft other
places, he had a palazzo at command, and was provided with table,
coach, and all other accommoda-

F   tions.

tions. While he was at this capital, he made ACIS and GALATEA, the words Italian, and the Mufic different from ours. It was compofed at the requeft of DONNA LAURA, whether a Portugueze or a Spanifh Princefs, I will not be certain. But the pomp and magnificence of this lady fhould feem to fpeak her of Spanifh extraction. For fhe lived, acted, and converfed with a ftate truly regal.

How HANDEL executed his tafk, we may guefs from what he has fince produced on the fame and other fubjects, under all the difadvantages of a language lefs foft and fonorous, and of Dramas conftructed without art or judgment, order or confiftency.

While he was at Naples he received invitations from moft of the
prin-

principal perfons who lived within
reach of that capital; and lucky
was he efteemed, who could engage
him fooneft, and detain him longeft.
After he quitted Naples, he made
a fecond vifit to Florence, Rome,
and Venice. Meeting with many
of his friends, he made fome ftay
at each of thofe places. The whole
time of his abode in Italy was fix
years. During this interval he had
made abundance of Mufic, and
fome in almoft every fpecies of
compofition. Thefe early fruits of
his ftudies would doubtlefs be vaft
curiofities could they now be met
with. The lovers of the art would
regard them with fomething of the
fame veneration, which the Literati
would pay to the precious remains
of a Livy, a Cæsar, or a Tacitus! Indeed the few fragments of
thofe pieces which have come to

F 2   our

our hands, ferve only to increafe our concern for the parts which have perifhed. And when the Reader is informed, that the two firft Movements of HANDEL's feventh Suite in the 1ft Vol. of his Leffons formerly ftood for the Overture in his famous Opera of AGRIPPINA; he will be lefs furprifed at the extravagant admiration of a Venetian audience, than at this effort of his genius before he was well nineteen. From fuch a fpecimen, he will form fome judgment of the work itfelf: he will be the more anxious for his other juvenile productions, fome of which are probably loft, and the reft only to be met with among the few Virtuofi, whofe enthufiaftic veneration for all that is truly great and excellent in its kind, hath acquired them that title; and of whom it is difficult

cult to fay, whether they are more
active and indefatigable in the
fearch of fuch treafure, or more
careful and vigilant in the guard-
ing of it.

HANDEL having now been long
enough in Italy effectually to anfwer the purpofe of his going thither, began to think of returning
to his native country. Not that
he intended this to be the end of
his travels ; for his curiofity was
not yet allay'd, nor likely to be fo
while there was any mufical court
which he had not feen. HANOVER
was the firft he ftopped at. STEF-
FANI was there, and had met with
favour and encouragement equal,
if poffible, to his fingular defert.
This perfon (whofe character is ele-
gantly fketched by a lover of his
Art and friend to his memory) he

F 3   had

had feen at Venice, the place of his
nativity. Such an acquaintance he
was glad to renew : for STEFFANI's
compofitions were excellent ; his
temper was exceedingly amiable ;
and his behaviour polite and genteel. Thofe who are inclined to
fee a fuller account of him, may
confult thofe Memoirs of his Life,
confifting indeed of a very few
pages, but fufficient to do him
great honour. We fhall foon have
occafion to mention him again, and
therefore fhall only add at prefent,
that he was Mafter of the Chapel to
his late MAJESTY, when he was
only Elector of Hanover. This
was an office and title highly cre-
ditable there, tho' far inferior to
thofe which he afterwards bore.

At Hanover there was alfo a
Nobleman who had taken great notice

tice of HANDEL in Italy, and who
did him great fervice (as will appear foon) when he came to ENG-
LAND for the fecond time. This
perfon was Baron KILMANSECK.
He introduced him at court, and
fo well recommended him to his
Electoral Highnefs, that he immediately offered him a penfion of
1500 Crowns per annum as an in-
ducement to ftay. Tho' fuch an
offer from a Prince of his character
was not to be neglected, HANDEL
loved liberty too well to accept it
haftily, and without referve. He
told the Baron how much he owed
to his kind and effectual recom-
mendation, as well as to his Highnefs's goodnefs and generofity. But
he alfo expreffed his apprehenfions
that the favour intended him would
hardly be confiftent either with the
promife he had actually made to vi-

F 4   fit

(72)

fit the court of the Elector Palatine, or with the refolution he had long taken to pafs over into England, for the fake of feeing that of LONDON.† Upon this objection, the Baron confulted his Highnefs's pleafure, and HANDEL was then acquainted, that neither his promife nor his refolution fhould be fuperfeded by his acceptance of the penfion propofed. He had leave to be abfent for a twelve-month or more, if he chofe it; and to go whitherfoever he pleafed. On thefe eafy conditions he thankfully accepted it.

To this handfome penfion the place of Chapel-mafter was foon after added, on the voluntary refignation of

† It feems he had received ftrong invitations to England from the Duke of Manchefter.

of TIFFANI. He thought such an office not perfectly confiftent with the high titles of Bifhop and Ambaffador, with which he was now invefted. And he was glad of this, or any other opportunity of obliging HANDEL. Notwithftanding the new favour conferred upon him, he was ftill in poffeffion of the privilege before allowed him, to perform his engagements, and purfue his travels. He confidered it as his firft and principal engagement to pay a vifit to his Mother at Hall. Her extreme old-age, and total blindnefs, tho' they promifed him but a melancholy interview, rendered this inftance of his duty and regard the more neceffary. When he had paid his refpects to his relations and friends (among whom his old Mafter ZACKAW was by no means forgot)

got) he set out for DUSSELDORP. The
Elector Palatine was much pleased
with the punctual performance of
his promise, but as much disap-
pointed to find that he was engaged elsewhere. At parting he made
him a present of a fine set of
wrought plate for a desert, and in
such a manner as added greatly to
its value.

From Dusseldorp he made the
best of his way through HOLLAND
and embarqued for ENGLAND. It
was in the winter of the year 1710,
when he arrived at LONDON, one of
the most memorable years of that
longest, but most prosperous war
(next to the present) which England had ever waged with a foreign
power. For during this period
scarce a mail arrived from Holland,
which

which did not bring fome frefh account of victories or advantages
gained by the Englifh Hero over
the armies of a Monarch, but lately
the terror of Europe, tho' now the
fcorn of every Dutch Burgomafter.
Nothing indeed feemed wanting to
compleat the national felicity, but
a perfon capable of charming down,
by the magic of his melody, that
evil fpirit of faction and party,
which fortune feems, at this time,
to have conjured up, as it were in
pure pity to her former favourite,
the afflicted LEWIS ! But HANDEL,
great as he was, could not do for
England, what David did for Saul.
The fame fpirit which had fo often
appeared in the courfe of the war,
prefided at the congrefs for peace.
The Mufic which HANDEL compofed on the completion of it, will
be

be mentioned elfewhere. In the mean time, it may not be amifs to fay a word or two on the ftate of Mufic at this his firft coming into England.

Excepting a few good compofi-tions in the church ftyle, and of a very old date, I am afraid there was little to boaft of, which we could call our own. At this time Operas were a fort of new acquain-tance, but began to be eftablifhed in the affections of the Nobility, many of whom had heard and ad-mired performances of this kind in the country which gave them birth. But the conduct of them here, *i. e.* all that regards the drama, or plan, including alfo the machinery, fcenes, and decorations, was foolifh and ab-furd almoft beyond imagination.

The

The laſt Pope but one was ſo exceedingly entertained with Mr. AD-
DISON's humourous account of this
curious management, that on reading his papers relating to it, he
laughed till he ſhook his ſides. Mr.
ADDISON ſeems, a little unfairly, to
impute this vitiated taſte to the
growing fondneſs for every thing
that was Italian. It is far from
impoſſible, that the Manager might
have found this taſte eſtabliſhed
here, and have been obliged to
conform to it. Who or what the
Compoſers were, we are not informed; nor is it very material to
enquire. For, from the account of
the commencement of the Italian
Opera here, as we find it in the 18th
Nº of the SPECTATOR, it is plain,
that, what with the confuſion of
languages, and the tranſpoſition of
paſſions

paſſions and ſentiments owing to
that cauſe, the beſt Compoſer could
hardly be diſtinguiſhed from the
worſt. The arrival of HANDEL
put an end to this reign of nonſenſe.

The report of his uncommon abilities had been conveyed to England
before his arrival, and through various channels. Some perſons here
had ſeen him in Italy, and others
during his reſidence at Hanover.
He was ſoon introduced at Court,
and honoured with marks of the
Queen's favour. Many of the nobility were impatient for an Opera
of his compoſing. To gratify this
eagerneſs, RINALDO, the firſt he
made in England, was finiſhed in
a fortnight's time. The words of
the Opera are by ROSSI, the firſt
ſen-

fentence of whofe preface is quoted
by the Spectator. This contains a
fort of panegyric on his own poetry, for which however he has
foon after the modefty to make
an apology. As it is fomewhat
curious, I fhall prefent the reader
with a little fpecimen of it.

" Gradifci, ti prego, difcretto
lettore, quefta mia rapida fatica, e
fe non merita le tue lodi, almeno
non privarla del tuo compatimen-
to, chi dirò più tofto guiftizia per
un tempo così riftretto: poiche il
Signer Hendel, Orfeo del noftro
fecolo, nel porla in Mufica, a pe-
na mi diede tempo di fcrivere; e
viddi, con mio grande ftupore, in
due fole fettimane armonizata al
maggior grado di perfezzione un
Opera intiera."

The

The fubject-matter of this Opera was furnifhed to ROSSI by the late Mr. AARON HILL, who alfo gave the publick an Englifh verfion of it. We learn from his preface, that at this time the Theatre at the Hay-Market was under his direction. And it appears from the account of his life prefixed to the laft edition of his dramatic works, that the year before he was manager of that at Drury-Lane. The character of this perfon feems to have been almoft as fingular as his adventures. Born of a good family, and endowed with fome natural talents, he might perhaps have arrived at that eminence to which he afpired, could he have confined himfelf to any fingle purfuit. But he was one of thofe active and enterprifing fpirits, that attempt every thing, and, for want of dif-

7   cerning

cerning their proper province, bring nothing to perfection. He travelled much, read much, and wrote much; and all, as it fhould feem, to very little purpofe. His intimate acquaintance with the moft eminent perfons of an age fo fruitful in *beaux Efprits*, inflamed his natural ardour to diftinguifh himfelf in the *belles Lettres*. He fancied that he was deftined to be a great Poet, and the high compliments he received from one, who was really fuch, confirmed him in that error. Whether this doth not create fome doubt of that fincerity and plain-dealing, on which Mr. POPE piqued himfelf fo much, I leave to be determined by thofe, who underftand the motives on which he acted. His noble friend had been equally lavifh in his praifes of Mr. HILL, and

G   the

the grounds of Mr. POPE's quarrel with both, or rather, of their quarrel with him, were juft the fame. When he found it neceffary to be more temperate in his commendations, this honeft referve was called ill treatment. Among authors there is nothing fo common as thefe effects of extravagant, or ill-placed approbation.

From Poetry to Mufic the paffage was natural and eafy. But from compofing Dramas to be fet, to the extracting oil from Beechnuts, was a tranfition quite peculiar to fuch a verfatile genius as Mr. HILL. The connexion betwixt the orcheftra and the alembic it is difficult to difcover.

To return to our account of RINALDO. In this Opera the famous NI-

NICOLINI fung. Its fuccefs was very
great, and his engagements at Hanover the fubject of much concern
with the lovers of Mufic. For
when he could return to England, or whether he could at
all, was yet very uncertain. His
Playing was thought as extraordinary as his Mufic. One of the
principal performers here ufed to
fpeak of it with aftonifhment,
as far tranfcending that of any
perfon he had ever known, and as
quite peculiar to himfelf. Another,
who had affected to difbelieve the
reports of his abilities before he
came, was heard to fay, from a too
great confidence in his own, " Let
" him come ! we'll Handle him,
" I warrant ye ! " There would
be no excufe for recording fo poor
a pun, if any words could be
found, capable of conveying the

cha-

character of the speaker with equal force and clearness. But the moment he heard HANDEL on the organ, this great man in his own eye shrunk into nothing.

He had now been a full twelvemonth in England, and it was time for him to think of returning to Hanover. When he took leave of the Queen at her court, and expressed his sense of the favours conferred on him, her Majesty was pleased to add to them by large presents, and to intimate her desire of seeing him again. Not a little flattered with such marks of approbation from so illustrious a personage, he promised to return, the moment he could obtain permission from the Prince, in whose service he was retained.

Soon

Soon after his return to Hanover he made twelve chamber Duettos for the practice of the late
Queen, then electoral Princefs.
The character of thefe is well
known to the judges in Mufic.
The words for them were written
by the Abbate MAURO HORTENSIO,
who had not difdained on other
occafions to minifter to the mafters
of harmony.

Befides thefe Duettos (a fpecies
of compofition of which the Princefs and court were particularly
fond) he compofed variety of other
things for voices and inftruments.

Towards the end of the year
1712, he obtained leave of the
Elector to make a fecond vifit to
England, on condition that he engaged

gaged to return within a reafonable time.

It was not many months after his arrival at LONDON that the peace of Utrecht was brought to a conclufion. Each year of this memorable reign had been fo crowded with heroic atchievements and grand events, that the poets and painters of our ifland feem to have funk, as it were, under the load of matter, which had been heaped upon them. And had our muficians been thought equal to the tafk, a foreigner would hardly have been applied to for the fong of triumph and thankfgiving, which was now wanted. The illuftrious family which had taken HANDEL into its patronage, had not only been deeply concerned, but highly diftinguifhed, in the

course

courfe of the war. The military talents, and perfonal bravery of its members had contributed to its profperous iffue. And not only the auguft houfe of Hanover, but moft of the proteftant Princes of the country to which he was indebted for his birth and education, had concurred in the reduction of that overgrown power, which long had menaced their religion and liberty. Thefe circumftances produced that particular fort of intereft and attachment, which, when joined to the dignity and importance of a fubject, difpofe an artift to the utmoft exertion of his powers. No performance can be thoroughly excellent, unlefs it is wrought *con amore*, as the Italians exprefs it. HANDEL, it muft be owned, had all thefe advantages. And it is not too much,

G 4   perhaps

perhaps it is too little to fay, that the work was anfwerable to them. But let the grand TE DEUM AND JUBILATE fpeak for themfelves! Our bufinefs is not to play the panegyrift, but the hiftorian.

The great character of the Operas which HANDEL had made in Italy and Germany, and the remembrance of RINALDO joined with the poor proceedings at the Haymarket, made the nobility very defirous that he might again be employed in compofing for that theatre. To their applications her Majefty was pleafed to add the weight of her own authority; and, as a teftimony of her regard to his merit, fettled upon him a penfion for life of 200 *l. per Annum.*

This

This act of the royal bounty
was the more extraordinary, as his
foreign engagements were not unknown.

Of the feveral Operas which he
made during this period fome account will be given in another
place. The time had again elapfed
to which the leave he had obtained, could in reafon be extended. But whether he was afraid of
repaffing the fea, or whether he
had contracted an affection for the
diet of the land he was in; fo it
was, that the promife he had given
at his coming away, had fome-
how flipt out of his memory.

On the death of the Queen in
1714, his late Majefty came over.
HANDEL, confcious how ill he had
deferved at the hands of his gra-

I   cious

cious patron, now invited to the throne of thefe kingdoms by all the friends of our happy and free conftitution, did not dare to fhew himfelf at court. To account for his delay in returning to his office, was no eafy matter. To make an excufe for the non-performance of his promife, was impoffible. From this ugly fituation he was foon relieved by better luck than perhaps he deferved. It happened that his noble friend Baron Kilmanfeck was here. He, with fome others among the nobility, contrived a method for reinftating him in the favour of his Majefty; the clemency of whofe nature was foon experienced by greater perfons on a much more trying occafion.

The King was perfuaded to form a party on the water. HANDEL

was

was apprifed of the defign, and advifed to prepare fome Mufic for
that occafion. It was performed
and conducted by himfelf, unknown
to his Majefty, whofe pleafure on
hearing it was equal to his furprife.
He was impatient to know whofe
it was, and how this entertainment came to be provided without
his knowledge. The Baron then
produced the delinquent, and afked leave to prefent him to his Majefty, as one that was too confcious
of his fault to attempt an excufe
for it ; but fincerely defirous to at-
tone for the fame by all poffible
demonftrations of duty, fubmiffion,
and gratitude, could · he but hope
that his Majefty, in his great goodnefs, would be pleafed to accept
them. This interceffion was accepted without any difficulty. HAN-
DEL was reftored to favour, and his
Mufic

Mufic honoured with the higheſt expreſſions of the royal approbation. As a token of it, the King was pleaſed to add a penſion for life of 200 *l.* a year to that which Queen ANNE had before given him. Some years after, when he was employed to teach the young Princeſſes, another penſion of the fame value was added to the former by her late Majeſty.

In the year 1715, he made the Opera of AMADIGE, as appears from the liſt annexed. I cannot find that he was employed in making any others between this time and the year 1720, excepting thoſe of TESEO and PASTOR FIDO: for tho' they have no dates to inform us with certainty when they were compoſed, they are known to have been among his earlieſt productions

of

of this kind, and muft have been performed in fome part of the interval above-mentioned.

During the three firft years of it, he was chiefly, if not conftantly, at the Earl of BURLINGTON's. The character of this nobleman, as a fcholar and virtuofo, is univerfally known. As Mr. POPE was very intimate with his Lordfhip, it frequently happened that he and HANDEL were together at his table. After the latter had played fome of the fineft things he ever compofed, Mr. POPE * declared,

* The Poet one day afked his friend Dr. ARBUTHNOT, of whofe knowledge in Mufic he had a high idea, What was his real opinion in regard to HANDEL as a Mafter of that fcience? The Doctor immediately replied, "Conceive the higheft that you can of his abilities, and they are much beyond any thing that you *can* conceive."

clared, that they gave him no fort
of pleafure ; that his ears were of
that untoward make, and reprobate
caft, as to receive his Mufic, which
he was perfuaded was the beft that
could be, with as much indifference as the airs of a common bal-
lad.   A perfon of his excellent un-
derftanding, it is hard to fufpect of
affectation.   And yet it is as hard to
conceive, how an ear fo perfectly
attentive to all the delicacies of
rhythm and poetical numbers, fhould
be totally infenfible to the charms
of mufical founds.   An attentive-
nefs too, which was as difcernible
in his manner of reading, as it is
in his method of writing.   But
perhaps the extravagant and inju-
dicious praifes, which the paffio-
nate admirers of the Art are apt to
beftow on fuch occafions, might
provoke one of his fatyric turn to

I   exprefs

exprefs himfelf more ftrongly than
he would otherwife have done.
Perhaps too, a Genius fo fond of
exploring characters, and fo emi-
nently fkilled in drawing them,
might think fuch an Artift as HAN-
DEL a proper fubject for experi-
ments in this way. The greateft
talents are often accompanied with
the greateft weaknefles. But the
Bard was much deceived if he imagined him weak enough to be mor-
tified by a declaration, which,
whether real or pretended, deferved not the leaft regard. HANDEL
minded it juft as much as POPE
would have done a like affurance
from *him* with refpect to Poems,
which all the world befides have
agreed to admire.

The remaining two years he
fpent at CANNONS, a place which
was

was then in all its glory, but remarkable for having much more
of art than nature, and much more
coft than art. Of the Mufic he
made for the Chapel there, fome
account will be given in another place. Whether HANDEL was
provided as a mere implement of
grandeur, or *chofen* from motives
of a fuperior kind, it is not for us
to determine. This one may ven-
ture to affert, that the having fuch
a Compofer, was an inftance of
real magnificence, fuch as no private perfon, or fubject; nay, fuch
as no prince or potentate on the
earth could at that time pretend
to.

During the laft year of his refi-
dence at Cannons, a project was
formed by the Nobility for erecting
an academy at the Haymarket.
The

The intention of this mufical Society, was to fecure to themfelves a
conftant fupply of Operas to be
compofed by HANDEL, and performed under his direction. For
this end a fubfcription was fet on
foot : and as his late Majefty was
pleafed to let his name appear at
the head of it, the Society was dig-
nified with the title of the Royal
Academy. The fum fubfcribed
being very large, † it was intended
to continue for fourteen years certain. But as yet it was in its em-
brio-ftate, being not fully formed
till a year or two after.

HANDEL therefore, after he quitted his employment at Cannons,
was advifed to go over to DRESDEN
in queft of Singers. Here he en-

H   gaged

† The KING fubfcribed 1000 *l.* and the Nobility 40,000 *l.*

gaged SENESINO and DURISTANTI, whom he brought over with him to ENGLAND.

At this time BUONONCINI and ATTILIO compofed for the Opera, and had a ftrong party in their favour. Great reafon they faw to be jealous of fuch a rival as HANDEL, and all the intereft they had was employed to decry his Mufic, and hinder him from coming to the Haymarket : but thefe attempts were defeated by the powerful affociation above-mentioned, at whofe defire he had juft been to Drefden for Singers.

In the year 1720, he obtained leave to perform his Opera of RADAMISTO. If perfons who are now living, and who were prefent at that performance may be credited,

the

the applaufe it received was almoft
as extravagant as his AGRIPPINA
had excited : the crowds and tu-
mults of the houfe at Venice were
hardly equal to thofe at LON-
DON. In fo fplendid and fafhionable an affembly of ladies (to
the excellence of their tafte we
muft impute it) there was no fha-
dow of form, or ceremony, fcarce
indeed any appearance of order or
regularity, politenefs or decency.
Many, who had forc'd their way
into the houfe with an impetuo-
fity but ill fuited to their rank and
fex, actually fainted through the
exceffive heat and clofenefs of it.
Several gentlemen were turned
back, who had offered forty fhil-
lings for a feat in the gallery, after
having defpaired of getting any in
the pit or boxes.

H 2 But,

But, it may be thought, that
the great excellence of SENESINO,
both as to voice and action, might
have a confiderable fhare in the
wonderful impreffions made upon
the audience. For, by virtue of
great advantages in the reprefenta-
tion, many performances of little
or no value, have not only paffed,
but been well received.—To the
ladies efpecially, the merits of SE-
NESINO would be much more ob-
vious, than thofe of HANDEL.—
Perhaps they would. That *all*
depended on the Compofer, I
am as far from afferting, as I am
from believing that any other
perfon could have fhewn fuch a
finger to equal advantage. Let
any impartial and competent judge
confider, whether it is likely that
the whole mufical world could
have

have afforded a compofer befides himfelf, capable of furnifhing Se-nesino with fuch a fong, as that of Ombra Cara in the very Opera before us.

The great fuccefs of it matur'd the project before concerted for eftablifhing an academy. For it could not be effected at once, as a confiderable number of great per-fons had been inftrumental in bringing over Buononcini and At-tilio. And thefe foreigners they were the more unwilling to aban-don, becaufe they really had abilities in their profeffion. Perhaps the con-tefts ran as high on both fides, as if the object of them had been much more important. Yet I cannot agree with fome, who think them of no importance, and treat them as ridiculous. Thofe who thought

H 3   their

their honour engaged to fupport the old Compofers; who really preferred them to HANDEL; or fancied that it was a defect of humanity, or an act of injuftice to difcard them, not becaufe they were unfit for their office, but becaufe another foreigner was come, who was thought to be fitter; — had furely a right to intereft themfelves warmly in their defence, at a time when they were fo much in want of affiftance.

And thofe, on the other hand, might as reafonably join in oppofing them, who were firmly convinced of HANDEL's great fuperiority; and who thought it for the honour of the nation to inlift in its fervice the moft eminent artifts. The old ones, in their opinion, had no right to complain of any preference

3   given

given to another, provided they
were duly paid for the time they
had been engaged. When difputes
are carried on with any heat or
violence, it is ufually taken for
granted, that both fides are in the
wrong. But thefe qualities fo difagreeable in their operation, are
often falutary in their effects. Ill
as things may feem to be managed
with them, it is poffible they might
be managed worfe without them.
For thefe eager enquiries, and warm
debates concerning what is fitteft
to be chofen and preferred, lead
us to the knowledge of what is
beft and moft perfect in the kind.
By lighting up the flame of emulation in the breafts of contending
artifts, they contribute to the ad-
vancement of the art. Deftroy
thefe workings of paffion, and

there

there is an end of patriots, poets, and virtuofos.

Perhaps therefore the ufes of quarrelling may compenfate for all its inconveniences. But if not, the art of quarrelling, without lofing one's temper, is, I fear, too difficult for even courts to teach or practife.—But I wander from my fubject.

Such then was the ftate of things in the year 1720, at the time RA-DAMISTO was performed. The fucceeding winter brought this mufical diforder to its crifis. In order to terminate all matters in controverfy, it was agreed to put them on this fair iffue. The fe-veral parties concerned were to be jointly employed in making an Opera, in which each of them was

3

to

to take a diſtinct act. And he, who by the general ſuffrage, ſhould be allowed to have given the beſt proofs of his abilities, was to be put into poſſeſſion of the houſe. The propoſal was accepted, whether from choice, or neceſſity, I cannot ſay. The event was anſwerable to the expectations of HANDEL's friends. His act was the laſt, and the ſuperiority of it ſo very manifeſt, that' there was not the leaſt pretence for any further doubts or diſputes. I ſhould have mentioned, that as each made an overture, as well as an act, the affair ſeemed to be decided even by the overture with which HANDEL's began. The name of the Opera was MUZIO SCÆVOLA *.

The

* For further particulars of the overture in this Opera, ſee the note to page 44.

The academy being now firmly
eftablifhed, and HANDEL appointed
Compofer to it, all things went on
profperoufly for a courfe of between
nine and ten years. And this may
juftly be called the period of mufical glory, whether we confider
the performances or the performers,
moft certainly not to be furpaffed,
if equalled, in any age or country.
The names and dates of the Operas
exhibited within this memorable
interval, may be found in their re-
gular feries by turning to the catalogue. And fome brief and general account of their character is
given in the obfervations at the end
of it.

The perfect authority which
HANDEL maintained over the fingers
and the band, or rather the total
fub-

fubjection in which he held them,
was of more confequence than can
well be imagined. It was the
chief means of preferving that order and decorum, that union and
tranquillity, which feldom are found
to fubfift for any long continuance
in mufical Societies. Indeed, all
Societies, like the animal body,
feem to carry in their very frame
and frabric, the feeds of their own
diffolution. This happens fooner
or later, only as thofe are forward-
ed or retarded by different caufes.

SENESINO, who, from his firft
appearance, had taken deep root,
and had long been growing in the
affections of thofe, whofe right to
dominion the moft civilized nations have ever acknowledged, began to feel his ftrength and importance. He felt them fo much, that
what

what he had hitherto regarded as legal government, now appeared to him in the light of downright tyranny. HANDEL, perceiving that he was grown lefs tractable and obfequious, refolved to fubdue thefe Italian humours, not by lenitives, but fharp corrofives. To *manage* him he difdained ; to controul him with a high-hand, he in vain attempted. The one was perfectly refractory ; the other was equally outrageous. In fhort, matters had proceeded fo far, that there were no hopes of an accommodation. The merits of the quarrel I know nothing of. Whatever they were, the Nobility would not confent to his defign of parting with SENESINO, and HANDEL was determined to have no farther concerns with him. FAUSTINA and CUZZONI, as if feized with the contagion of difcord,

discord, started questions of superiority, and urged their respective
claims to it with an eagerness and
acrimony, which occasioned a total dis-union betwixt them.

And thus the Academy, after it
had continued in the most flourish-
ing state for upwards of nine years,
was at once dissolved.

The late Laureat, who, now and
then, has some strokes of humour,
(for dulness too hath its lucid intervals) diverts himself much on the
subject of these musical frays. The
unlucky effects of them at the marriage of the late Duke of Parma,
he describes with that pert kind of
pleasantry, that native *gaillardise*
which attended him through life.
The fondness for Italian Singers,
he thinks unaccountable: the ex-

pence

pence and trouble they occafion,
exorbitant and ridiculous. He calls
them coftly Canary-birds; and on
their behaviour at the marriage folemnity juft mentioned above, la-
ments as follows, " What a pity it
is, that thefe froward Miffes and
Mafters of Mufic, had not been engaged to entertain the court of
fome King of Morocco, that could
have known a good Opera from a
bad one! With how much eafe
would fuch a Director have brought
them to better order ?" — But, had
he known any thing of the true †
fpirit of Handel, he would not have
wifhed them under better government.

† Having one day fome words with Cuzzoni on her refufing to fing *Falfa imagine* in
Ottone; Oh! Madame, (faid he) je fçais
bien que Vous êtes une veritable Diableffe:
mais je Vous ferai fçavoir, moi, que je fuis Beel-
zebub le *Chéf* des Diables. With this he took
her up by the waift, and, if fhe made any more
words,

ment. It is true they mutinied, and
rebelled at laſt. But the ſlaves of
Aſiatic and of African Monarchs,
have often done as much.

He remained inflexible in his re-
ſolution to puniſh SENESINO for re-
fuſing him that ſubmiſſion, which
he had been uſed to receive, and
which he thought he had a right to
demand : but a little pliability
would have ſaved him abundance
of trouble. The vacancy made by
the removal of ſuch a Singer was
not eaſily ſupplied. The umbrage
which he had given to many of the
Nobility, by his implacable reſent-
ments

words, ſwore that he would fling her out of the
window.
    It is to be noted, that this was formerly one
of the methods of executing criminals in ſome
parts of Germany ; a proceſs not unlike that
of the Tarpeian rock, and probably derived
from it.

ments againſt a perſon whoſe talents they ſo much admired, was likely to create him a dangerous oppoſition. For, tho' he continued at the Hay-market, yet, in the heat of theſe animoſities, a great part of his audience would melt away. New Singers muſt be ſought, and could not be had any nearer than Italy. The buſineſs of chuſing, and engaging them, could not be diſpatched by a deputy. And the party offended might improve the opportunity of his abſence to his diſadvantage.

In ſpite of all theſe diſcouragements, to Italy he went, as ſoon as he had ſettled an agreement with HEIDEGGAR to carry on Operas in conjunction with him. The agreement was for the ſhort term of
three

three years, and so settled as to
subsist only from year to year.

On his arrival at Rome, he received a very friendly and obliging
letter of invitation from cardinal
COLONNA, with a promise of a very
fine picture of his Eminence. But,
hearing that the Pretender was then
at the Cardinal's, he prudently de-
clined accepting both the invitation
and the picture.

After a short stay in Italy, he
returned with STRADA, BERNACHI,
FABRI, BERTOLDI, and others. Being thus embarqued on a new bottom, he went on in conjunction
with HEIDEGGER, but not with that
even and prosperous gale which had
wafted him so smoothly and plea-
santly through the nine preceding
years: for about the time of the

I   sepa-

feparation at the Hay-market, occafioned by the difagreement between HANDEL and his Singers,
many of the Nobility raifed a new
fubfcription in order to carry on another Opera at Lincoln's-inn-fields,
in which they could have Singers
and Compofers of their own chu-
fing. With this view they fent for
PORPORA, FARINELLI, and others.
The former was author of feveral
Cantatas which were much admired, and gave great fatisfaction to
the perfons who employed him.
The latter charmed all hearers by
his exquifite voice, which he knew
how to manage to the beft advantage. Tho' HANDEL bore up with
great fpirit and firmnefs againft
this oppofition, he foon felt the
effects of it; and yet, at the expi-
ration of the three years partnerfhip
with HEIDEGGER, he ventured to
continue

continue Operas at the Hay-market
for one year on his own bottom.
Finding this attempt no way likely
to fucceed, he left the Hay-market,
and on the return of the adverfe
party to it, removed to the vacant
theatre at Lincoln's-inn-fields. Here
he continued but a little while ; for
he confidered that the tide of oppofition was now at its full heighth,
and that to ftem it, his own ftrength,
fuperior as it was, might not be fufficient. The little tafte he had already had of adverfity, leffened that
felf-confidence which fuccefs is apt
to infpire. He found that it was
not the neceffary confequence of
great abilities, and that without
prudence the greateft may be almoft annihilated in the opinions of
men. But it is a principal part of
prudence, to command our temper
on any trial we may chance to re-

I 2   ceive ;

ceive ; a part of it which, to fay
the truth, he never practifed or pro-
feffed. This omiffion involved him
in misfortunes, which taught him
another part of prudence (if it muft
be called fo) which he never ought
to have practifed, much lefs profef-
fed, that of confulting his intereft at
the expence of his art.

He now removed to Convent-
garden, and entered into a partnerfhip with RICH, the mafter of that
houfe. HASSE and PORPORA were
the Compofers at the Hay-market.
When the former was invited over,
it is remarkable, that the firft queftion he afked, was, whether HAN-
DEL was dead. Being anfwered in
the negative, he refufed to come,
from a perfuafion, that where his
countryman was (for they were both
Saxons by birth) no other perfon of
the

the fame profeffion was likely to
make any figure. He could not
believe that in a nation which had
always been famous for fenfe and
difcernment, the credit of fuch an
artift as HANDEL could ever be impaired. However, this myftery was
explained to him in fuch a manner,
and this explanation accompanied
by fuch offers, that at length he got
the better of his fcruples, and confented to be engaged. He is remarkable for his fine elevated air,
with hardly fo much as the fhew
of harmony to fupport it. And this
may ferve not only for a character
of HASSE-in particular, but of the
Italians in general, at the time we
are fpeaking of. The oppofition in
which they were engaged againft
HANDEL, made him look upon that
merit in his antagonifts with much
indifference, and upon this defect

I 3   with

with ſtill more contempt. He carried his contempt ſo far, as to endeavour to be as unlike them as poſſible. He could have vanquiſhed
his opponents at their own weapons; but he had the ſenſe to diſ-
cover, that the offended and prejudiced ſide would never have acknowledged his victory however de-
ciſive; and that his new friends,
for want of underſtanding the nature and uſe of ſuch weapons, would
not have diſcerned it however obvi-
ous. From hence he gradually fell
into that too cloſe and particular
attachment to the harmony, which
ſometimes led him to neglect the
melody, even where it ought moſt
to be regarded, I mean in Vocal
Muſic. A farther account of the
cauſes and conſequences of this
omiſſion, may be found in the obſervations on his works.

In

In the fummer of the year 1733,
he made a tour to OXFORD, where
there was a public Act, at which
he performed his Oratorio of ATHA-
LIAH, compofed for that folemnity.
By this journey the damages he had
fuffered in his fortune were fomewhat repaired, and his reputation
more firmly eftablifhed.   The next
winter his Opera of ARIANNA
was performed at Convent-garden,
while another of the fame name,
compofed by PORPORA, was acted at the Hay-market. POLY-
PHEMO by the fame perfon, and
ARTAXERXES by HASSE, gained
great applaufe there foon after.
Though HANDEL had fome good
Singers, none of them could be
compared to FARINELLI, who drew
all the world to the Hay-market.
And it foon appeared that the re-

lifh

lifh of the Englifh for Mufic, was
not ftrong enough to fupport two
Operas at a time. There were but
few perfons of any other clafs, befides that of the Nobility, who had
much knowledge of the Italian,
any notion of fuch compofitions,
or confequently any real pleafure
in hearing them. Thofe among
the middling and lower orders,
whom affectation or curiofity had
drawn to the Theatre at his firft
fetting out in conjunction with
Rich, fell off by degrees. His
expences in providing Singers, and
in other preparations, had been
very large ; and his profits were no
way proportionate to fuch charges.
At the end of three or four years,
inftead of having acquired fuch an
addition to his fortune, as from his
care, induftry, and abilities, he
had reafon to expect, he was obliged

ged to draw out of the funds almoſt all that he was worth, in order to anſwer the demands upon
him. This upſhot put an end for
the preſent to all muſical entertainments at Convent-garden, and almoſt put an end to the author of
them. The violence of his paſſions
made ſuch a diſaſter operate the
more terribly.

The obſervation that misfortunes
rarely come ſingle, was verified in
HANDEL. His fortune was not
more impaired, than his health and
his underſtanding. His right-arm
was become uſeleſs to him, from a
ſtroke of the palſy ; and how greatly his ſenſes were diſordered at intervals, for a long time, appeared
from an hundred inſtances, which
are better forgotten than recorded.
The moſt violent deviations from

I   reaſon,

reafon, are ufually feen when the ftrongeft faculties happen to be thrown out of courfe.

In this melancholic ftate, it was in vain for him to think of any frefh projects for retrieving his affairs. His firft concern was how to repair his conftitution. But tho' he had the beft advice, and tho' the neceffity of following it was urged to him in the moft friendly manner, it was with the utmoft difficulty that he was prevailed on to do what was proper, when it was any way difagreeable. For this reafon it was thought beft for him to have recourfe to the vapor-baths of Aix la Chapelle, over which he fat near three times as long as hath ever been the practice. Whoever knows any thing of the nature of thofe baths, will, from this inftance,

form

form fome idea of his furprifing conftitution. His fweats were profufe
beyond what can well be imagined.
His cure, from the manner as well
as from the quicknefs, with which
it was wrought, paffed with the
Nuns for a miracle. When, but a
few hours from the time of his quit-
ting the bath, they heard him at
the organ in the principal church
as well as convent, playing in a
manner fo much beyond any they
had ever been ufed to, fuch a conclufion in fuch perfons was natural
enough. Tho' his bufinefs was
fo foon difpatched, and his cure
judged to be thoroughly effected,
he thought it prudent to continue at
Aix about fix weeks, which is the
fhorteft period ufually allotted for
bad cafes.

Soon after his return to London
in 1736, his ALEXANDER's FEAST

4   was

was performed at Convent-Garden, and was well received.

After much mifmanagement, and various mifunderftandings at the Hay-market, the glories of that theatre feemed quite extinct. Lord MIDDLESEX, defirous of feeing the Opera reftored to its former fplendor, undertook the direction of it, and applied to HANDEL, as the fitteft perfon to fupply it with compofitions. He made two Operas for his Lordfhip, FARAMONDO and ALESSANDRO SEVERO; the laft of which was a Pafticcio, and performed, as well as the other, in the year 1737. For thefe he received 1000*l.* Had he been difpofed to make any conceffions, his friends might eafily have effected a reconciliation between him and his opponents. All parties would in that cafe have been glad

glad to have feen him again at the Hay-market; for at this time all the fources of Opera-mufic feem to have been drained to the very dregs. The fenfe of his abilities, the prefent exigency in which they were fo much wanted, the recollection of his loffes and fufferings; time itfelf, which as it confumes many valuable things, fo it often happily wears out perfonal refentments:——In fhort, every thing feemed to concur, and nothing was wanting to infure his future profperity, excepting a fpirit which knew how to yield on proper occafions. From a fingle benefit made for him at the Haymarket in the year 1738, from which he is faid to have received 1500 *l.* it is eafy to guefs what might have been done to recover his affairs. But he was fo averfe

to

to fubfcription-engagements, that
he refolved to be for the future on
a quite different footing. No pro-
fpects of advantage could tempt him
to court thofe by whom he thought
he had been injured and oppreffed.
Full of thefe lofty fentiments, he
returned to Convent-Garden, where
he performed a few more Operas,
the dates of which may be found in
the catalogue. Finding that the
tafte of his audience was naturally
averfe to this fpecies of compofition, he now introduced another,
more fuited to the native gravity
and folidity of the Englifh, tho'
borrowed from the *concert fpiri-
tuel* of their volatile neighbours on
the continent. Esther was made
originally for the Duke of Chandois, about a year after Acis *and*
Galatea. After it had been performed at Cannons, it was played
at

at the Crown and Anchor; and this indeed is faid to have firft furnifhed the hint for bringing Oratorios on the ftage. As the moft remarkable characters, events, and occurrences contained in the holy fcriptures, are intended to be reprefented in thefe folemn pieces, it is plainly of their nature to be acted, as well as fung, and accompanied. But the very facrednefs and folemnity of the fubjects treated, made even the fetting them to Mufic appear to fome perfons little lefs than a prophanation. What ftrengthened this opinion was probably this, that moft of the relations which are the fubject matter of Operas are taken from prophane and fabulous hiftory. And though Mufic was allowed to lend its affiftance in places of worfhip ; yet it feemed to be a dangerous innovation to allow it the further

pri-

privilege of canvaffing in full form
religious fubjects in places of entertainment. It feemed to be form-
ing a fort of alliance between
things ufually confidered in a
ftate of natural oppofition, the
church and theatre. In times when
narrow notions were more in vogue,
and when even men of fenfe were
governed rather by appearances
than by realities, Oratorios would
not have been tolerated. In thefe
happier days the influence of prejudice was not indeed quite ftrong
enough to exclude thefe noble performances, yet it is even ftill ftrong
enough to fpoil them. For are not
the very fame arguments which prevailed for admitting Oratorios fufficient to juftify the acting them?

Would not action and gefticula-
tion accommodated to the fituation
and

and fentiments, joined with dreffes conformable to the characters reprefented, render the reprefentations more expreffive and perfect, and confequently the entertainment much more rational and improving *. Provided no improper characters were introduced, (a thing eafy to be obviated) what other inconvenience could poffibly refult from the further allowance here contended for, it is hard to imagine. But this is fpoken with perfect fubmiffion to the proper judges.

About

RACINE'S ESTHER and ATHALIAH fet by LULLI, and performed at the convent of St. Cyr, by Order of Madame DE MAINTENON, had all the advantages of theatrical imitation. Indeed the beft performance, if properly dramatic, without the helps of fuitable action, and proper dreffes, muft needs lofe a confiderable part of that force and clearnefs, that life and fpirit, which refult from a full and perfect exhibition.

K

About the year 1729, or 1730, ESTHER and DEBORAH had been performed at the Hay-market with good fuccefs; with much better indeed than he met with at Convent-Garden, when he tried them there but a few years after. He feems not fufficiently to have confidered the rifques which he ran in this new undertaking. The diftance of this theatre from thofe parts of the town where the nobility chiefly re-fide; the relics of the oppofition not yet extinct, though fomewhat abated; a ftyle little fuited as yet to the apprehenfions of the gene-rality;—thefe, and probably fome other caufes, may have concurred to render his attempt inaufpicious in its commencement. Too much accuftomed to difappointments to be eafily difpirited, he continued

thefe

thefe new entertainments, fo excel--
lently adapted to the feafon of
the year in which they are exhibited, till the beginning of the year
1741. But at this time his affairs
again carried fo ill an afpect, that
he found it neceffary to try the
event of another peregrination. He
hoped to find that favour and en--
couragement in a diftant capital,
which London feemed to refufe
him. For even his MESSIAH had
met with a cold reception. Either
the fenfe of mufical excellence was
become fo weak, or the power of
prejudice fo ftrong, that all the
efforts of his unparalleled genius
and induftry proved ineffectual.

DUBLIN has always been famous
for the gaiety and fplendor of its
court, the opulence and fpirit of
its principal inhabitants, the valour

of

of its military, and the genius of
its learned men. Where fuch things
were held in efteem he rightly
reckoned, that he could not better
pave the way to his fuccefs, than
by fetting out with a ftriking inftance and public act of generofity
and benevolence. The firft ftep
that he made, was to perform his
Messiah for the benefit of the city-
prifon. Such a defign drew together
not only all the lovers of Mufic,
but all the friends of humanity.
There was a peculiar propriety in
this defign from the fubject of the
Oratorio itfelf; and there was a
peculiar grace in it from the fituation of Handel's affairs. They
were brought into a better pofture
by his journey to Dublin, where
he ftaid between eight and nine
months. The reception that he
met with, at the fame time that it
fhewed

shewed the strong sense which the
Irish had of his extraordinary merit, conveyed a kind of tacit re-
proach on all those on the other
side of the water, who had enlisted
in the opposition against him. Mr.
Pope in the fourth book of the
Dunciad has related this passage of
his history. A poor phantom, which
is made to represent the genius of
the modern Italian Opera, ex-
presses her apprehensions, and gives
her instructions to Dulness, already
alarmed for her own safety. The
lines are well known, but, for their
strong characteristic imagery, deserve to be quoted in this place.
They are as follows,

But soon, ah soon, rebellion will commence,
If Music meanly borrows aid from Sense :
Strong in new arms, lo! giant Handel stands,
Like bold Briarius with his hundred hands ;

To

To ftir, to roufe, to fhake the foul he comes,
And Jove's own thunders follow Mars's
  drums.
Arreft him, emprefs ; or you fleep no more —
She heard,—and drove him to the Hibernian
  fhore.

At his return to London in
1741-2, the minds of moft men
were much more difpofed in his
favour. He immediately recom-
menced his Oratorios at Convent-
Garden. Sampson was the firft he
performed. And now (to ufe the
exprefiive phrafe of Tacitus) *blan-
diebatur cæptis fortuna* ; Fortune
feemed rather to court and carefs,
than to countenance and fupport
him. This return was the æra of
his profperity. Indeed, in the year
1743, he had fome return of his
paralytic diforder ; and the year
after fell under the heavy difplea-
fure of a certain fafhionable lady.
                               She

She exerted all her influence to fpirit up a new oppofition againft him.
But the world could not long be made
to believe that her card-affemblies
were fuch proper entertainments for
Lent, as his Oratorios. It is needlefs to enlarge upon particulars
which are eafily remembered, or
to give a minute account of
things generally known. It is
fufficient juft to touch on the moft
remarkable. What is very much
fo, his MESSIAH which had before
been received with fo much indifference, became from this time the
favourite Oratorio. As in the year
1741, it was applied to the relief
of perfons expofed to all the mife-
ries of perpetual confinement; it
was afterwards confecrated to the
fervice of the moft innocent, moft
helplefs, and moft diftreffed part
of the human fpecies. The Found-

K 4   ling

ling Hofpital originally refted on
the flender foundation of private
benefactions. At a time when this
inftitution was yet in its infancy;
when all men feemed to be convinced of its utility; when nothing
was at all problematical but the
poffibility of fupporting it;—HAN-
DEL formed the noble refolution to
lend his affiftance, and perform his
MESSIAH annually for its benefit.
The fums raifed by each performance were very confiderable, and
certainly of great confequence in
fuch a crifis of affairs. But what
was of much greater, was the magic
of his name, and the univerfal character of his facred Drama. By thefe
vaft numbers of the nobility and
gentry were drawn to the hofpital;
and many, who, at the firft, had been
contented with barely approving
the defign, were afterwards warmly
engaged

engaged in promoting it. In confequence of this refort, the attention of the nation was alfo drawn
more forcibly to what was indeed
the natural object of it. So that it
may truly be affirmed, that one of
the nobleft and moft extenfive cha-
rities that ever was planned by the
wifdom, or projected by the piety
of men, in fome degree owes its
continuance, as well as profperity,
to the patronage of HANDEL.

The very fuccefsful application
of this wonderful production of his
genius to fo beneficent a purpofe,
reflected equal honour on the Artift and the Art.

He continued his Oratorios with
uninterrupted fuccefs, and unrival-
led glory, till within eight days of
his death : the laft was performed
on

on the 6th of April, and he expired on Saturday the 14th of April 1759. He was buried the 20th by Dr. PEARCE, Bifhop of Rochefter, in Weftminfter-abbey, where, by his own order, and at his own expence, a monument is to be erected to his memory.

In the year 1751, a gutta ferena deprived him of his fight. This misfortune funk him for a time into the deepeft defpondency. He could not reft until he had undergone fome operations as fruitlefs as they were painful. Finding it no longer poffible for him to manage alone, he fent to Mr. SMITH to defire that he would play for him, and affift him in conducting the Oratorios.

His

His faculties remained in their full vigour almoſt to the hour of his diſſolution, as appeared from Songs and Choruſſes, and other Compoſitions, which from the date of them, may almoſt be conſidered as his parting words, his laſt accents! This muſt appear the more ſurpriſing, when it is remembered to how great a degree his mind was diſordered, at times, towards the latter part of his life.

His health had been declining apace for ſeveral months before his death. He was very ſenſible of its approach, and refuſed to be flattered by any hopes of a recovery. One circumſtance was very ominous, I mean the total loſs of appetite, which was come upon him, and which muſt prove more pernicious

cious to a perfon always habituated,
as he had been, to an uncommon
portion of food and nourifhment.
Thofe who have blamed him for an
exceffive indulgence in this loweft
of gratifications, ought to have
confidered, that the peculiarities of
his conftitution were as great as
thofe of his character. Luxury and
intemperance are relative ideas, and
depend on other circumftances befides thofe of quantity and quality.
It would be as unreafonable to confine HANDEL to the fare and allowance of common men, as to expect
that a London merchant fhould
live like a Swifs mechanic. Not
that I would abfolve him from *all*
blame on this article. He certainly
paid more attention to it, than is
becoming in any man : but it is
fome excufe, that Nature had given
him fo vigorous a conftitution, fo

exquifite

exquifite a palate, and fo craving
an appetite; and that fortune en-
abled him to obey thefe calls, to
fatisfy thefe demands of Nature.
They were really fuch. For befides the feveral circumftances juft
alledged, there is yet another in
his favour; I mean his inceffant
and intenfe application to the ftudies of his profeffion. This rendered conftant and large fupplies
of nourifhment the more neceffary
to recruit his exhaufted fpirits. Had
he hurt his health or his fortune
by indulgences of this kind, they
would have been vicious: as he
did not, they were at moft inde-
corous. As they have been fo much
the fubject of converfation and plea-
fantry, to have taken no notice of
them, might have looked like affectation. But it would be folly to
enter into the particulars of this

part

part of his hiſtory, and contrary to
the deſign of the foregoing ſheets,
which is only " to give the Reader
thoſe parts of his † character, as a
Man, that any way tend to open
and explain his character as an Ar-
tiſt." So that the connection between this account of his life, and
the following obſervations on his
works, is cloſer than, at firſt ſight,
may be imagined. How far the
materials

† It was thought better to leave the Reader
to collect his character from the LIFE itſelf,
than to attempt the drawing of it in form : a
practice which has not ſucceeded over-much,
even where it is moſt neceſſary ; I mean in the
writings of Hiſtorians. Truth hath ſeldom been
ſo much as conſulted in theſe ſtudied repreſen-
tations. That conſtant and uniform oppoſition
of the ſeveral parts, which, with much force
and ſtraining, are made to tally with each
other, renders *moſt* characters only a more extended antitheſis, and is ſcarce ever found really to exiſt in *any*. Yet often is this ſpurious
brood of affectation and wit, palmed upon the
world for the genuine offspring of education
and nature.

I

materials for the former may be
worth the digefting, can fairly be
determined only by examining them
in this view. How far they are
well digefted, is another queftion,
which every one will determine for
himfelf, excepting the perfon employed in this attempt. But for
his induftry in collecting them, fuch
as they are, they would probably
have been loft in the courfe of a
few years. He has nothing to add,
but his fincere wifhes, that every
Artift, who is truly deferving in his
profeffion, may meet with a perfon
equally defirous of doing juftice to
his memory.

F I N I S.

CATALOGUE

OF THE

WORKS

OF

George Frederic Handel.

I Think that the works of HAN-
DEL may conveniently be diftri-
buted into three claffes, *viz.*

1.

CHURCH-MUSIC.

2.

THEATRICAL MUSIC.

3.

CHAMBER-MUSIC.

And thefe again into ten inferior
or leffer claffes, *viz.*

1. ANTHEMS *and* TE DEUMS.
2. ORATORIOS.
3. OPERAS.
4. CONCERTOS, *for* Inftruments.
5. SONATAS, *for two* Violins *and*
   a Bafs.

6. LESSONS, *for the* Harpsichord.

7. CHAMBER-DUETTOS.

8. TERZETTOS.

9. CANTATAS *and* PASTORAL PIECES.

10. OCCASIONAL, *or* FESTAL PIECES.

In the following catalogue there are several compositions, *viz.* ALLEGRO ED IL PENSEROSO, TRIUMPH *of* TIME *and* TRUTH, *&c.* which are placed among the Oratorios, because they were performed as such, but do not properly belong to that species. Indeed they cannot be said to fall under any of the classes above described. However they are not of consequence enough to form a distinct one among the lesser, any more than the WATER-MUSIC among the larger.

As

As to the TRIUMPH *of* TIME *and* TRUTH, great part of the Mufic is the fame with that of IL TRIONFO DEL TEMPO, made at Rome many years before, revived in 1757, and performed only once at the Haymarket [in Italian] about the time the Oratorios firft began.

A great quantity of Mufic, not mentioned in the Catalogue, was made in Italy and Germany. How much of it is yet in being, is not known. Two chefts-full were left at HAMBURGH, befides fome at HANOVER, and fome at HALL.

THEATRICAL MUSIC.

OPERAS.

ALMERIA, made and performed at Hamburgh.

FLORINDA, Hamburgh.

NERONE, ditto.

RODERIGO, Florence.

AGRIPPINA, Venice.

IL TRIONFO DEL TEMPO, Rome.
  [Serenata.]

ACIGE e GALATEA, Naples. [Sere-
  nata.]

RINALDO, London, 1710.

TESEO, ditto.

AMADIGE, ditto, 1715.

PASTOR FIDO, ditto.

RADAMISTO, ditto. 1720.

MUZIO SCÆVOLA, ditto, 23 March,
  1721.

OTTONE, ditto, 10 Auguſt, 1722.

FLORIDANTE, ditto. ——— 1723.

FLAVIO, ditto.— 7 May, 1723.

JULIO CÆSARE, ditto—- 1723.

TAMERLANE, ditto, 23 July 1724.

RODELINDA, ditto, 20 Jan. 1725.

SCIPIONE, ditto, 2 March 1726.

ALESSANDRO, ditto, 11 April 1726.

RICARDO, London, 16 May 1727.
AMMETO, ditto, 16 May 1727.
SIROE, ditto, 5 February 1728.
PTOLOMEO, ditto, 19 April 1728.
LOTARIO, ditto, 16 Nov. 1729.
PARTENOPE, ditto, 12 Feb. 1730.
PORO, ditto, 26 January, 1731.
SOSARME, ditto, 4 February 1732.
ORLANDO, ditto, 20 Nov. 1732.
EZIO, ditto, 1733.
ARIANNA, ditto, 5 October 1733.
ARIODANTE, ditto, 24 Oct. 1734.
ALCINA, ditto, 8 April 1735.
*ATALANTA, ditto, 20 April 1736.
GIUSTINO, ditto, 7 Septemb. 1736.
ARMINIO, ditto, 30 Octob. 1736.
BERENICE, ditto, 18 Jan. 1737.
FARAMONDO, ditto, 24 Dec. 1737.
ALESSANDRO SEVERO, ditto. [Pa-
fticcio.]
SERSE, ditto, 6 February 1738.

* Performed at the Princefs of ORANGE's
wedding.

* IMENEO, ditto, 10 Oct. 1740.
DIEDAMIA, London, 20 Oct. 1740.

ORATORIOS.

DEBORAH, 21 Feb. 1733.
ESTHER.
ATHALIAH, 7 June, 1733.
ALEXANDER'S FEAST, 17 Jan. 1736.
ISRAEL *in* EGYPT, 11 Oct. 1738.
ALLEGRO ED IL PENSEROSO, 1739.
SAUL, 1740.
MESSIAH, 12 April, 1741.
SAMPSON, 12 Oct. 1742.
† SEMELE, 4 July, 1743.
SUSANNAH, 9 August, 1743.
BELSHAZZAR.
HERCULES, 17 August 1744.

OCCA-

* Performed on occasion of his late ROYAL HIGHNESS the PRINCE of WALES's wedding.

† An English Opera, but called an Oratorio, and performed as such at Covent-Garden. The words of it by CONGREVE.

† Occasional Oratorio, 1745.
Judas Macchabæus, 11 Aug. 1746.
Joseph, 1746.
Alexander Balus, 30 June 1747.
Joshua, 18 Aug. 1747.
Solomon, 13 June 1748.
Theodora, 18 July 1749.
Jeptha, 20 Aug. 1751.
Triumph *of* Time *and* Truth.

SERENATAS.

Il Trionfo del Tempo, Rome.
Acige e Galatea, Naples.
*Acis *and* Galatea, for the Duke of Chandois, about the year 1721.
Parnasso in Festa, [an Italian entertainment, sung at the Haymarket.]
Choice of Hercules.

Church-

† Performed on occasion of the victory gained at Culloden, by his Royal Highness the Duke of Cumberland.

* The words of this piece wrote by Mr. Gay.

CHURCH-MUSIC.

A grand Te Deum and Jubilate
for the peace of Utrecht, 1713.
Four Coronation Anthems, 1727.
Several Anthems made for the Duke
of Chandois between 1717, and
1720.
Several more; as a Funeral Service
for her late MAJESTY Queen
CAROLINE; in all about twenty-
three.
Three more Te Deums; one of
which was on the occasion of
the victory at DETTINGEN.

CHAMBER-MUSIC.

Cantatas, [the greatest part made
at Hanover, and other places
abroad; in all about 200.
Chamber-Duettos, [twelve made at
Hanover, and two after he came
to England.]

Serenatas,

Serenatas, [moſt of them made a-
broad, and ſome few at his firſt
coming to England, one of which
was for Queen ANNE, and performed at St. James's, but afterwards loſt.]

INSTRUMENTAL-MUSIC.

Muſic for the Water.
Concertos for different Inſtruments.
Sonatas for two Violins and a Baſs.
Harpſichord-Leſſons.
Twelve grand Concertos.
Twelve ditto for the Organ.

OBSERVATIONS

ON THE

WORKS

OF

George Frederic Handel.

BEFORE we enter on the examination of HANDEL's works, it is neceſſary to ſettle the meaning of ſome words, which, on other ſubjects have been uſed with no great care, but never perhaps with ſo little as when they have been applied to Muſic. It is of conſequence to underſtand them well: for, whether we would explain the grounds, or diſtinguiſh the kinds, or eſtimate the degrees of muſical excellence, recourſe muſt ſtill be had to theſe expreſſions. A clear notion of the ſubject to which they are applied, will direct us to their true meaning.

Muſic

Mufic is founded on eftablifhed
rules and principles. There are
certain relations and proportions
which fubfift between founds, and
certain effeds, which are conftantly
and regularly † produced by their
different union, arrangement, and
combination. The rules are derived from experience and obfervation, which inform us what particular fyftem or difpofition of founds
will produce the moft pleafing effeds. A clear comprehenfion of
thofe rules, and the ability to ap-
ply them, are called *knowledge* :
and

† It is almoft needlefs to make exceptions
with regard to thofe who diflike Mufic, or who
never attend to its effeds. For (as the Abbé
Du Bos fays) Il eft des hommes tellement in-
fenfibles à la Mufique, & dont l'oreille (pour
me fervir de cette expreffion) eft tellement
eloignée du cœur, que les chants les plus na-
turels ne les touchent pas.

and this alone, without any great
fhare either of *invention* or *tafte*,
may make a tolerable Compofer.
But either of thefe joined with it,
forms a mafter.

The mafters may be diftinguifhed
into two claffes, as their principal
merit confifts in *invention* or *tafte*.
The former of thefe feems to con-
fift in the quick inveftigation of
new, or hitherto-unperceived relations ; in the combining thefe relations after an unufual manner, or
according to a different order ; and
in the happy application of them
to particular fubjects, efpecially to
fuch as are of an important or in-
terefting nature.

Thofe who have an *inventive*
genius will depart from the common rules, and pleafe us the more

M   by

by fuch deviations. Thefe muft of
courfe be confidered as bold ftrokes,
or daring flights of fancy. Such
paffages are not founded on rules,
but are themfelves the foundation
of new rules.

On the other hand, they who
have *tafte*, or a nice difcernment
of the minuter circumftances that
pleafe, will polifh and improve the
inventions of others. Thefe will
adhere ftrictly to rules, and even
make them more ftrict.

Hence we may difcern the reafon why great *invention* and perfect *tafte* are feldom, or never united, altho' either the one or the
other may *meet* with *knowledge*.

Hence too we may conclude,
that the merit of HANDEL's Mufic
will

will be leaft difcerned by the lovers of elegance and correctnefs.
They are fhocked with every defect of this fort, while their very
character hinders them from enter-
ing into thofe excellencies of a
higher nature, in which he fo much
furpaffes all other Muficians : excellencies, which are hardly confiftent with a conftant regard to
thofe minuter circumftances, on
which beauty depends. As *tafte*
implies a natural fenfibility, and
an habitual attention to thefe very
circumftances, all neglects of them
fall under its jurifdiction. But as
this faculty is of a tender and ti-
mid nature, it is apt to confider
thofe bolder ftrokes and rougher
dafhes which genius delights in, either as coarfe, or as extravagant.
However, when it attempts to cha-
ftife or correct fuch paffages, it

miftakes

miftakes its province. Art is *here*
not only ufelefs, but dangerous. It
may eafily deftroy originality, tho'
it cannot create elegance ; which if
it *could* be had, would be ill pur-
chafed at the expence of the other.
For the generality of mankind have
not enough of delicacy to be much
affected with minute inftances of
beauty ; but yet are fo formed, as to
be tranfported with every the leaft
mark of grandeur and fublimity.

What gives me the fuller affurance in the truth of thefe principles, is their agreement with the
following obfervations, which a Gentleman, who is a perfect mafter of
the fubject, was fo good as to com-
municate to me. The obfervations
are as follows :

" As

" As party and prejudice have been carried pretty high, on the one fide in favour of HANDEL, and on the other in favour of the Italians, I fhall endeavour to confider this affair with the impartiality it requires, and fettle, to the beft of my judgment, the merits on both fides.

The tafte in Mufic both of the Germans and the Italians, is fuited to the different characters of the two nations. That of the firft is rough and martial; and their Mufic confifts of ftrong effects produced, without much delicacy, by the rattle of a number of inftruments. The Italians, from their ftrong and lively feelings, have endeavoured in their Mufic to exprefs all the agitations of the foul, from the moft

M 3　　　delicate

delicate fenfations of love, to the moft violent effects of hatred and defpair ; and this in a great degree by the modulation of a fingle part.

HANDEL formed his tafte upon that of his countrymen, but by the greatnefs and fublimity of his genius, he has worked up fuch effects as are aftonifhing. Some of the beft Italian mafters, by the delicacy of their modulation, have fo deeply entered into all the different fenfations of the human heart, that they may almoft be faid to have the paffions of mankind at their command ; at leaft of that part of mankind, whofe lively feelings are fomewhat raifed to a pitch with their own.

When we confider two kinds of Mufic fo very different in character,

ter, as that of Handel, and that
of the beſt Italians, and both carried to ſo great a degree of perfection, we cannot be ſurpriſed at ſee-
ing ſuch warm advocates for each.
Handel's Muſic muſt be allowed
to have had ſome advantages over
theirs, independent of its real merit. The fulneſs, ſtrength, and
ſpirit of his Muſic, is wonderfully
well ſuited to the common ſenſa-
tions of mankind, which muſt be
rouſed a little † roughly, and are
not of a caſt to be eaſily worked

M 4   upon

† It is only Handel's *general* character that
is here oppoſed to that of the Italians. For
though the caſt of his mind was *more* towards
the great and ſublime than any *other* ſtyle, yet
he ſometimes excels the Italians themſelves
even in the paſſionate and pathetic. This appears from particular inſtances, which we ſhall
have occaſion to cite preſently; and from
others which might be cited. That theſe have
been overlooked, is probably owing to the
many inſtances of a contrary kind in his Ora-
tories and elſewhere.

upon by delicacies. Thus he takes
in all the unprejudiced part of mankind. For in his fublime ftrokes,
of which he has many, he acts as
powerfully upon the moft Know-
ing, as upon the Ignorant. Another advantage which he has over
the Italians, is owing to themfelves.
The quantity of bad Mufic we have
had from Italy, prejudices many
againft the good. And here it may
not be amifs to fay fomething of
the prefent ftate of the Italian
Mufic.

The old Mufic, fuch as it was
in the time of PALESTRINO, and
thofe excellent Compofers in the
Church ftyle, was performed by a
number of voices: the harmony
was full and varied ; and the effects were produced by the able
management of their fugues and
imita-

imitations through all the parts.
This required great skill in Music,
as well as genius : so that at that
time no man could set up for a
Compofer, without a very profound
knowledge of the rules of compofition. It happened, as it naturally
muft when the ftudy of Mufic en-
gages men of great abilities, both
as to genius and knowledge, that
improvements were conftantly ari-
fing from one quarter or another.
By this means the art of modulating
a fingle voice, fo as to exprefs the
various paffions and affections, was
every day gaining ground, till VINCI
and PERGOLESI carried it in fome
of their Songs to the higheft pitch
we can as yet have any idea of.
With this exquifite expreffion in the
voice, they have fhewn equal skill
in the management of the inftruments that accompany it. For their

I   inftru-

inftrumental parts are fo judici-
oufly contrived, that they are conftantly adding new beauties to the
Song-part without ever overwhelm-
ing it.

I cannot but lament that the
Song-mufic which we have from
Italy, has been dwindling ever fince
their time. And from the prefent
fituation of things, I think there is
but little reafon to hope that it will
rife again. The Italian Compofers
have two things ftrongly againft
them, and which I conceive to be
the caufe of all the trifling, frothy
Mufic we have at this time. The
one is, the little time they have for
compofing. For as foon as any rifing genius has given fome ftriking
proof of his abilities, the Managers
of almoft every Opera in Italy, want
to engage him to compofe for them.
The

The young fellow thinks his reputation is eftablifhed, and endeavours
to make the moſt of it, by undertaking to compoſe as much as it is
poſſible to do in the time. This
obliges him to write down any
thing that firſt preſents itſelf: and
thus his Opera is chiefly made up
of old worn-out paſſages haſtily
put together, without any new turn
of expreſſion, or harmony. Almoſt every Compoſer of genius in
Italy, is an inſtance of this. But
the moſt ſtriking inſtance I know
is JOMELLI, who has in ſome things
ſhewn himſelf to be equal to any
Compoſer that has gone before him,
while in many others he does not
appear even above the common
rank. The other difficulty the
Italian Opera-compoſers have to
ſtruggle with, is the undue influence of the Singers over them. A
good

good Singer (which is equally applicable to both the fexes) feldom
fails to make fuch a party in his favour, as it would not be prudent
in the Compofer to difoblige. This
in fome degree puts him under the
Singer's direction in relation to his
own Songs; which is in fact the
being directed in his compofitions
by a perfon that knows very little
of Mufic, and that wants to fhine
by playing all the tricks he has been
able either to invent or to learn.

This being the prefent fituation
of the Italian Compofers, it is not
furprifing that their compofitions
fhould be fo thin and flimfy. For
it is hardly to be expected, that a
Compofer will be at the pains to do
all he can, when the low price he
is to have for his Opera, will hardly find him bread, if he has fpent
much

much time upon it ; and when he may risque both bread and reputation by displeasing a favourite Singer.

From all that has been said, I would conclude, that both those who indiscriminately condemn HANDEL's compositions, and those who in like manner condemn the Italian Music, are equally to blame as prejudiced or ignorant deciders. And I would recommend it to all true lovers of Music, to examine with candor, and I may even add, with some degree of reverence, the compositions of men, whose great abilities in their profession do honour to human nature. I think it is highly probable, that whatever delicacies appear in HANDEL's Music, are owing to his journey into Italy ; and likewise that the Italians

lians are much indebted to him for their management of the inftrumental parts that accompany the voice; in which indeed fome few of them have fucceeded admirably well. And as fome proof of HANDEL's influence in Italy, it is, I believe, an undoubted fact, that French-horns were never ufed there as an accompaniment to the voice, till HANDEL introduced them.

But however well fome of the Italians may have fucceeded in the management of the inftrumental parts in their Song-mufic, there is one point in which HANDEL ftands alone, and in which he may poffibly never be equalled; I mean in the inftrumental parts of his Choruffes, and full Church-mufic. In thefe he has given innumerable inftances of an unbounded genius.

In

In ſhort, there is ſuch a ſublimity
in many of the effects he has work'd
up by the combination of inſtruments and voices, that they ſeem
to be rather the effect of inſpira-
ration, than of knowledge in Muſic."

But in order to make a right
judgment of his abilities in Muſic,
attention muſt conſtantly be had to
its two different ſpecies, *viz.* the inſtrumental and vocal.

The excellence of the former
conſiſts in the ſtrength and fulneſs of its † harmony : that of the
latter

† This is to be underſtood with ſome limi-
tation. For it is not meant that the excellence
of Inſtrumental Muſic conſiſts *altogether* in the
ſtrength and fulneſs of its harmony ; but only
that this is the perfection of it as contradiſtin-
guiſhed from the Vocal. The Concertos of
Tartini,

latter in the delicacy and propriety of its melody.

Now that fulneſs of harmony, which is eſſential to the one, may in ſome caſes hurt, if it doth not deſtroy, the perfection of the other. Rousseau has developed this matter wonderfully well in his *Lettre ſur la Muſique Françoiſe*. And it is in this point that I think Handel is ſometimes faulty, and the beſt Italian maſters almoſt conſtantly right, although I do not carry my idea

Tartini, and of ſome other firſt-rate Compoſers for inſtruments are ſtrong proofs that the excellence of Inſtrumental Muſic ſhould not be confined to harmony alone. For the merit of thoſe pieces conſiſts ſtill more in the high and uncommon delicacy of the melody, than in the harmony, though excellent in its kind, and incomparably well contrived for the ſetting off and ſtrengthening the expreſſion of the principal part.

idea of their perfection quite so far
as ROUSSEAU does.

As Operas and Oratorios plainly
belong to the vocal class, the Recitative and Air must always be considered as the principal parts in such
performances. Yet in some of
HANDEL's, the Symphonies and Accompaniments, instead of shewing
those parts to advantage, have ab-
sorbed them, as it were, in their
own superior splendor. His uncommon strength in the instrumental way, which it was natural for
him to be fond of displaying, may
have been one reason for his falling
into this fault. Another perhaps
was the badness of some of his
Singers; for there never was an
Opera in which all of them were
good. A judicious Composer will
always take care that the worst

shall

ſhall have little to do. But unleſs
the inſtruments by their predomi-
nant harmony, fill up the vacui-
ties occaſioned by the abſence, or
thinneſs of the vocal parts, the attention of the audience muſt ne-
ceſſarily languiſh : an inconvenience evidently greater than that of
violating the rules of propriety, by
giving to the inſtruments more ſtreſs
than the ſubject will warrant.

It may alſo be added, that in ſo
long a performance as that of an
Opera, there muſt be many Airs in
different ſtyles, and on different
ſubjects. The fineſt modulations,
continued too long, or repeated too
often, would flatten upon the ear.
Here again recourſe muſt be had to
the inſtruments, which, by a little
over-acting their part, gain attention to thoſe Songs of a lower claſs,
which

which ferve to fet off and recommend the others. So that we muft
not wonder, if in HANDEL's old
Operas we meet with fome * Songs,
which, from the fulnefs of the parts,
appear to be almoft Concertos.

But how fhall we excufe for
thofe inftances of coarfenefs and
indelicacy which occur fo frequently in the Airs of his Oratorios? For
as the melody is a fundamental and
effential part in vocal Mufic, it
fhould feem that nothing can at-
tone for the neglect of it. The
beft Painter would be blamed,

N 2   fhould

* Yet in many others all the parts are fo
nicely adjufted, and fo well fuftained, that the
feveral inftruments in his Orcheftra, refemble
the feveral perfonages in a fine piece of hiftory-
painting, all engaged and interefted in the fame
fubject, and all concurring, in their different
fituations, to the furtherance and execution of
the principal defign.

should he draw off the attention
too much from the principal figure
in his piece, however perfect, by
the very high and exquisite finish-
ing of some inferior object: but
much more would he deserve to be
blamed, if he left that figure the
least finished, which all the rules
of his art required to be the most
so. Now in Music, though there
may sometimes be occasion, as we
have seen, for giving the instru-
ments the ascendancy over the voices; yet never should the Song-
parts be unmeaning or inexpressive,
much less coarse or ordinary.

To speak the plain truth, HAN-
DEL was not so excellent in Air,
where there is no strong character
to mark, or passion to express.
He had not the art, for which the
Italians have ever been remarkable,
the

the art of trifling with grace and delicacy. His turn was for greater things, in expreffing which it is hard to fay, whether he excelled moft in his Air, or in his Harmony. This may be proved even from his Oratorios, where he has failed the moft * and the ofteneft. But in his old Operas there are numberlefs inftances of his abilities in the vocal way, fuch as it would be difficult to parallel out of the greateft Ma-fters, whofe whole excellence lay in that particular fpecies. I will

N 3   only

* Some allowances muft be made for the difadvantages he was under from the Audi-ence, the Singers, and the Language, all of them changed for the worfe.

A gentleman whom he had defired to look over JUDAS MACCHABÆUS, having declared his opinion of it; Well, (faid HANDEL) to be fure you have picked out the beft Songs, but you take no notice of that which is to get me all the money; meaning the worft in the whole Oratorio.

only refer the Reader to a few
Songs in different ftyles, *viz.*

Ûn difprezzato affetto,⎫
         &   ⎬in OTTONE.
* Affanni del penfier,⎭
Ombra cara, in RADAMISTO.
Men fedele, ⎫
     &   ⎬in ALESSANDRO.
Il mio cor, ⎭

Here too he will fee, that tho',
in two of the Songs above-cited,
there is great employment for the
inftruments ; and though in all of
them the parts which they have to
execute, are exceedingly fine ; yet
they are fo contrived, as not to
eclipfe

---

* An eminent Mafter, who was not on good
terms with HANDEL, often declared the opinion he had of his abilities in very ftrong ex-
preffions. That great Bear (faid he) was certainly infpired when he made this Song. He
might have faid the fame with full as much
juftice of that which I have coupled with it.

eclipfe the air or melody. At the
fame time that they relieve the ear
by the beauty and variety of their
accords, they † affift the voice in
expreffing the particular action,

N 4   paffion,

---

† After all, the vocal fpecies is not more
indebted to the inftrumental, than this is to the
other. Many inftances might be produced to
confirm this affertion, from the compofitions
of different Mafters. But TARTINI's Mufic
may almoft be confidered as one continued inftance of it. All his melody is fo truly vocal
in its ftyle and character, that thofe parts of it
which do not exceed the compafs and powers
of a voice, one would almoft imagine were intended to be fung. His moft difficult paffages
bear the fame character, which was very appa-
rent, when they were executed by himfelf: and
all the Italians were fo ftrongly fenfible of this,
that in fpeaking of his manner of playing, they
often made ufe of the following expreffion, *non
fuona, canta fu'l violino.* The reafon why the
compofitions of this great Mafter are admired
by fo few people in Egland, is that the Performers of them neither enter into the true character of the Mufic, nor play it according to
the intention of its author. The more any
piece

paffion, or fentiment intended to be reprefented.

And here I may juft take notice, that the proper place for moft mu-fical imitations, is in the Symphonies and Accompaniments.   There are indeed fome few founds, which Na-ture herfelf employs to exprefs the ftronger emotions of the human heart, which the voice may imi-tate.   But it is common for the Ma-fters not only to forget the nature and * extent of this imitative power
in

piece of Mufic is delicate and expreffive, the more infipid and difagreeable muft it appear un-der a coarfe and unmeaning execution.   Juft as the moft delicate ftrokes of humour in co-medy, and the moft affecting turns of paffion in tragedy, will fuffer infinitely more from be-ing improperly read, than a common para-graph in a news-paper.

* See Mr. HARRIS's three treatifes, in which this point is difcuffed with great judgment and accuracy.

in Mufic, but alfo to miftake the
fubject on which to employ it. A
too clofe attachmment to fome particular words in a fentence, hath
often mifled them from the general
meaning of it. HANDEL himfelf,
from his imperfect acquaintance
with the Englifh language, has
fometimes fallen into thefe miftakes. A Compofer ought never
to pay this attention to fingle words,
excepting they have an uncommon
energy, and contain fome paffion
or fentiment. To do HANDEL
juftice, he is generally great and
mafterly, where the language and
poetry are well adapted to his purpofe. The Englifh tongue abounds
with monofyllables and confonants.
Tho' thefe cannot always be avoid-
ed, yet the writers of mufical dramas fhould always pick out fuch
as are the leaft harfh and difagreeable

able to the ear. The fame regard muſt be had to the ſentiments, as to the language. The more ſimple and natural they are, the more eaſily will Muſic expreſs them. There was a time (ſays Mr. ADDI-SON) when it was laid down as a maxim, that nothing was capable of being well ſet to Muſic, that was not nonſenſe. This ſatyr is equally juſt and beautiful. But tho' the ſenſe of ſuch productions cannot be too ſtrong, the poetry of them may be too fine. If it abounds with noble images, and high wrought deſcriptions, and contains little of character, ſentiment, or paſſion, the beſt Compoſer will have no opportunity of exerting his talents. Where there is no-thing capable of being expreſſed, all he can do is to entertain his audience with mere ornamental

paſſages

paffages of his own invention. But graces and flourifhes muft rife from the fubject of the compofition in which they are employed, juft as flowers and feftoons from the de-fign of the building. It is from their relation to the whole, that thefe minuter parts derive their value.

To return to our examination of HANDEL's works. In his Choruffes he is without a rival. That eafy, natural melody, and fine flowing air, which runs through them, is almoft as wonderful a peculiarity, as that perfect fulnefs and variety, amid which there feems however to be no part but what figures, and no note that could be fpared.

His Anthems are choral through-out, and fo excellent in their kind, that

that it would be difficult to conceive
any thing of human production that
is more fo. Thofe which he made
for the Duke of Chandois's chapel
are the leaft known, but far from
being among the leaft excellent.
It is true that in the admirable epiftle addreffed to Lord Burlington,
the two following lines, viz.

" Light quirks of mufic, broken and uneven,
Make the foul dance upon a jig to heaven;"

which are meant to expofe the
falfe tafte of fuch Mufic, as is either foreign to the fubject, or improper for the occafion, may appear to be levelled at HANDEL, as
he was employed in compofing for
the chapel of the nobleman, whofe
miftaken notions of magnificence
were fuppofed to be pointed at by
more circumftances than one in the
lines

lines immediately preceding thofe
I have quoted. But there are many
reafons, which make it utterly improbable that any Mufic of HAN-
del's is here intended. For though
Mr. POPE was no judge himfelf of
any productions on this fubject, yet
he had many friends who well underftood them ; and none indeed
better than the very lord, to whom
his epiftle is addreffed. Befides, the
opinion which he actually entertained of HANDEL's abilities, may
be gathered from thofe fine lines
upon him, which are quoted, in
his life, from the 4th book of the
DUNCIAD. It is however no way
improbable that the fame chapel
might have furnifhed inftances of
the egregious impropriety here ri-
diculed, after HANDEL ceafed to
compofe for it. But whether it
did or not, it was the Poet's bufinefs

nefs to go through the feveral inftances of a perverted tafte, in
which the fcene he made choice of
abounded perhaps more than any
other.

The reader will excufe this di-
greffion, as it feemed neceffary to
guard againft miftakes not lefs in-
jurious to the judgment of Pope
on the one hand, than to the honour of Handel on the other.

As his Oratorios are all, or moft
of them, on fcripture-fubjects, fo
the Choruffes in them are quite in
the church-ftyle; and it may be
faid without extravagance, that the
fublime ftrokes they abound with,
look more like the effects of illu-
mination, than of mere natural genius. Out of a multitude of examples which might be produced,

I will only remind the reader of
the few following in the single
Oratorio of MESSIAH, *viz.*

For unto us a child is born, &*c.*
Lift up your heads, O ye gates,&*c.*
Hallelujah, for the Lord God
omnipotent reigneth, &*c.*

After these vast efforts of genius,
we find him rising still higher in
the three * concluding Choruffes,
each of which furpaffes the preceding, till in the winding up of
the Amen, the ear is fill'd with
fuch a glow of harmony, as leaves
the mind in a kind of heavenly
extafy.

There are indeed but few perfons fufficiently verfed in Mufic,
to

---

* Beginning with, " Worthy is the lamb
that was flain."

4

to perceive either the particular
propriety and juftnefs, or the general union and confent, of all the
parts in thefe complicated pieces.
However, it is very remarkable that
fome perfons, on whom the fineft
modulations would have little or
no effect, have been greatly ftruck
with HANDEL's Choruffes. This
is probably owing to that grandeur
of conception, which predominates
in them; and which, as coming
purely from Nature, is the more
ftrongly, and the more generally
felt.

It is true, that, in the wonderful perfomance above-mentioned,
there are great inequalities, as in
moft of HANDEL's: but whoever
fhould examine it throughout, muft
confider him as a down-right pro-
digy. I ufe this expreffion becaufe
there

there are no words capable of conveying an idea of his character, unlefs indeed I was to repeat thofe
which Longinus has employed in
his defcription of Demosthenes,
every part of which is fo perfectly
applicable to Handel, that one
would almoft be perfuaded it was
intended for him †.

His excellence in another branch
of vocal Mufic, *viz*. the Recitative, might eafily be fhewn either
from his old Operas, or from the
fingle Oratorio above-mentioned.
For a fpecimen, the following paffages will be fufficient:

Comfort ye, comfort ye, my people,
    faith your God,   Messiah.

                                Alma

† See the conclufion of Longinus's 33d
Section.

O

Alma del gran POMPEO,
>   JULIO CÆSARE.

To which we may add, that grand
fcene of the death of BAJAZET in
Tamerlane.

Without attempting to explain
the caufes of that forcible expreffion, and overpowering pathos,
which breathe in thefe, and many
other paffages of his Recitative, I
will only alledge thefe effects of
Mufic, to fhew that its true ufe,
and greateft value, is to heighten
the natural impreffions of religion
and humanity.

The Duettos and Terzettos were
made at different times. Thofe
which he made abroad having never
been printed, are in very few hands,
and but little known. As they are
of

of a character fomewhat different
from his latter compofitions of the
fame kind, and in fome refpects
fuperior to them, they deferve particular notice. They were compofed in the vigour of his faculties,
not for the theatre, but for the
clofet. Nothing was to be facri-
ficed to the rude, undifcerning ear
of the multitude; nor were invention and harmony to be given
up for the poor purchafe of an
encore. The author had only himfelf to pleafe, or fcholars formed
by himfelf: and let any one judge
whether his compofition was not
likely to be the better for fuch
circumftances. Indeed, as might
well be expected, we find thefe
admirable productions free from
fuch marks of hafte and negligence, as are feen, and fhould in
all reafon be excufed, in the works

of

of length, which he has since
composed. When we complain
of these productions as frequently
defective with regard to taste and
delicacy, we should do well to re-
collect how little of either belongs
to that tribunal, before which their
merits were to be decided. But to
resume our examination of the
Duettos. It is as hard to characte-
rize these, as the other parts of
HANDEL's works. Though they
may be said to comprehend most
styles, yet the manly and the ner-
vous prevail upon the whole. Indeed, in some of them there is a
sweetness and delicacy of modulation not inferior to that of the
amiable STEFFANI; as in many
there is a spirit and majesty to
which he appears to have been a
stranger.

It

It was not to be diffembled that the manly caft of HANDEL's mind often led him into a kind of melody ill fuited to the voice; that he was apt to depart from the ftyle which the fpecies of compofition demanded, and run into paffages purely inftrumental. Yet fo admirable is the contrivance, and fo beautiful the modulation in fome of thefe pieces, where this deviation is moft confpicuous; that the beft judge of Mufic, who examines them as a critic, will hardly have the heart to execute his office; and, while the laws of it compel him to arraign the fault, will almoft be forry to fee it corrected. That all this may not appear to be faid at random, let us enter a little into the particulars.

The Duetto beginning, " *Am-* " *mirarvi io fono intento,*" is a

O 3   beau-

beautiful example of a ſtyle truly
vocal, and much reſembling that
of STEFFANI.

That beginning, " *Conſervate*,"
is another inſtance of the ſame
kind. The firſt movement of
" *Sono liete*," is another ; but the
laſt movement of the ſame is inſtrumental. Of this we have, in
a manner, the author's acknow-
ledgment ; for he introduced it afterwards, with ſome alteration, into
the Overture of JUDAS MACCHA-
BÆUS.

As examples of a ſpirited and
beautiful manner unknown to the
calm and eaſy STEFFANI, I ſhall
only mention, among many others,
" *Che vai penſando*," and " *Tacete*."

Among the Trios " *Quando non
hò più core*," is an inſtance of the
inſtru-

inftrumental ftyle, carried fo far, as to render the performance of it extremely difficult.

In fome parts of thefe pieces, but more particularly in the Terzettos, it is curious to obferve thofe vaft conceptions of the choral kind, pent up within the narrow limits of two or three parts; and ftruggling as it were, for that enlargement, which has fince permitted them to take their full fweep in the wide, and almoft unbounded province of *Chorus*. To fhew that this obfervation is not chimerical, it need only be recollected that one of the fineft Choruffes in the ALLEGRO, and that very artificial one with which ALEXANDER's FEAST concludes, were made out of two of thefe Trios.

Though the Duettos and Trios in his Operas and Oratorios are not

in

in general fo chafte, or of fo learned a caft, as thofe of which we
have juft been fpeaking, yet the
mufical reader will eafily call to
mind feveral of diftinguifhed beauty. Such are the famous Trio in
Acis and Galatea ;— the Duetto,
" *O death, where is thy fting,*" in
Messiah ; — " *From this dread
fcene,*" in Judas Macchabæus ;—
and " *Io t'abbraccio,*" in Rodelinda.

The only Serenata (properly fo
called) which he made here, was
Acis and Galatea ; and it is one
of the moft equal and perfect of all
his compofitions. From this we
may guefs at the merits of thofe
which are not extant. The Cantatas now remaining have been hitherto little examined. That of
Tarquin and Lucretia was made
at Rome, and its merits are much

3   better

better known in Italy than in England.

We have now run through his several productions in the vocal species ; and from this curfory examination I think it muft appear, that even where he is leaft excellent on the whole, he has given fuch frequent, and fuch ftrong proofs of his abilities, as place him on a level with the greateft Mafters, whofe whole ftrength lay in that particular fpecies.

In his Mufic for inftruments there are the fame marks of a great genius, and likewife fome inftances of great negligence. He often attended more to the effect of the whole, than to that artificial contexture of the parts, for which GEMINIANI is fo juftly admired.

In

In his Fugues and Overtures he
is quite original. The Style of
them is peculiar to himfelf, and no
way like that of any Mafter before
him. In the formation of thefe
pieces, knowledge and invention
feem to have contended for the
maftery.

Tho' no man ever introduced
fuch a number of inftruments, yet
in his Orcheftra not one is found
idle or infignificant. On the contrary, each hath fuch a figure and
character belonging to it, as feems
to render it not only proper and
ufeful, but neceffary and effential
to the performance. Even thofe
which are of the loweft order, and
leaft value, when confidered in
themfelves, from the artful and
judicious manner in which they
are introduced and employed, rife

into

into a kind of dignity and importance, of which by nature they
ſhould ſeem incapable.

Of his talents in compoſing for
a ſingle inſtrument, we need no
better proofs than are given us in
his Harpſichord-leſſons. The firſt
ſett, which were printed by his own
order, will always be held in the
higheſt eſteem, notwithſtanding
thoſe real improvements in the ſtyle
for leſſons which ſome Maſters have
ſince hit upon. HANDEL's have
one diſadvantage, owing entirely to
their peculiar excellence. The ſurpriſing fulneſs and activity of the
inner parts, increaſes the difficulty
of playing them to ſo great a degree, that few perſons are capable
of doing them juſtice. Indeed
there appears to be more work
in them than any one inſtrument
ſhould ſeem capable of diſpatch-
ing.   To

To conclude, there is in thefe and other parts of his works, fuch a fulnefs, force, and energy, that the harmony of HANDEL may always be compared to the antique figure of HERCULES, which feems to be nothing but mufcles and finews ; as his melody may often be likened to the VENUS of MEDICIS, which is all grace and delicacy.

Whatever fhall be thought of this attempt to do juftice to his memory, too much reafon there is for believing that the interefts of religion and humanity are not fo ftrongly guarded, or fo firmly fecured, as eafily to fpare thofe fuccours, or forego thofe affiftances which are miniftered to them from the elegant arts.

They

They refine and exalt our ideas of pleafure, which when rightly underftood, and properly purfued, is the very end of our exiftence. They improve and fettle our ideas of tafte ; which, when founded on folid and confiftent principles, explains the caufes, and heightens the effects, of whatever is beautiful or excellent, whether in the works of creation, or in the productions of human fkill.

They adorn and embellifh the face of Nature ; the talents of men they fharpen and invigorate ; the manners they civilize and polifh ; in a word, they foften the cares of life, and render its heavieft calamities much more fupportable by adding to the number of its innocent enjoyments.

The

The hopes of rendering fome
fervice to Mufic, and of fuggefting
fome hints which may poffibly give
rife to farther enquiries into this
difficult fcience, have induced me
to fubjoin to the foregoing lift of
HANDEL's works, fuch obfervations
upon them, as feemed to offer
themfelves in the courfe of this review. For if the obfervations are
juft, thofe who are mafters of the
fubject may be tempted to improve
and extend them ; and if they are
erroneous, the fame perfons are at
liberty to refute them.

At all events, fuch a view of the
various and valuable improvements
derived to Mufic from the inceffant
labours, and wonderful endowments
of one * man, may ferve to awaken
the

* There are but a few perfons, who have
carefully looked over, and are thoroughly acquainted with *all* the works of HANDEL, and
they

the attention of the Curious to thofe
new fources of beauty and fublimity
which may yet lie concealed in the
regions of harmony. It may alfo
ferve to put future Artifts on a more
careful ftudy of his compofitions in
every kind, and fo check the progrefs of thofe corruptions in tafte,
which in every period have threat-
ned deftruction to the Art, and in
none perhaps more than in the
* prefent.

Little
they only can be proper judges of his abilities.
Yet a fingle glimpfe of the Catalogue may en-
able us to guefs at the aftonifhing extent of his
genius : for he has not only ranged through the
whole compafs of his Art, but has given un-
queftionable proofs of his excellence in all the
branches of it.

* Our moft fafhionable Mufic of late years
carries hardly any appearance of knowledge
or invention, hardly indeed any traces of tafte
or judgment. Light and trivial Airs, upheld
by a thin and fhadowy Harmony ; an almoft
perpetual uniformity of ftyle, and famenefs of
fubject ; an endlefs repetition of the fame
move-

(208)

Little indeed are the hopes of ever equalling, much lefs of excelling fo vaft a Proficient in his own way: however, as there are fo many avenues to excellence ftill open, fo many paths to glory ftill untrod, it is hoped that the example of this illuftrious Foreigner will rather prove an incentive, than a difcouragement to the induftry and genius of our own countrymen.

movements and paffages, tho' worn to rags; the barren and beggarly expedient of Pafticcios fo often practifed;—fuch a decay as this in the ftate of Mufic, (I forbear to make thofe exceptions which the Judges of the Art will make for themfelves) fhould excite fome veneration for the works of HANDEL.

F I N I S.